WOW! WISDOM

❦

"What a privilege to have read *Wow! Wisdom*. It is heart-warming and uplifting; amusing and moving. Billy has a unique ability to illustrate wisdom's truths through a compelling cast of fascinating characters. Once begun, the book is difficult to put aside. It is both delightful and inspiring, and it makes one eager to discover the wisdom hidden in strange places and unlikely people."

Bishop Richard C. Looney, United Methodist Church, Retired,
Chattanooga, Tennessee

❦

"*Wow! Wisdom* stands out for its eloquent simplicity. In an accessible, human, and touching style, Billy reminds us to be mindful about the power of relationships. Each story represents real people doing ordinary things that have an extraordinary impact on the lives of people around them. Following each of Billy's authentic stories, you will find study questions to move you from observation to action. The questions remind all of us that wisdom challenges us to ask questions—to say, "I don't know" or "I'm not sure." When we question and listen, we become a better version of ourselves. Aristotle said, 'Knowing yourself is the beginning of all wisdom.' Billy's book will help you along the path to knowing yourself."

Steve Piscitelli, Author, Speaker, and Retired Professor
Atlantic Beach, Florida

❦

"*Wow! Wisdom* is a profound reminder of the power of God, who continually offers us the sacred in the everyday moments of our lives. Billy's authentic voice comes through with humor and thoughtfulness to remind us to take holy pauses in our moment-to-moment living to let God surprise us, amaze us, and inspire us."

Rev. Nancy K. Anderson, M.Div., ACPE Educator,
Manager of Clinical Pastoral Education, Spartanburg Regional
Spartanburg, South Carolina

WOW!

WISDOM

Stories from the Path of Life

Billy Hester

Author of Wow! Moments

Billy Hester Books, LLC / Savannah, Georgia

Wow! Wisdom
Stories from the Path of Life
by Billy Hester

Published by Billy Hester Books, LLC, Savannah, Georgia, USA
BillyHesterBooks.com
Printed by CreateSpace, An Amazon.com Company
Available from Amazon.com and other retail outlets

ISBN 978-0-9979-9811-5

This book is dedicated to my grandmothers,
Gladys Graham and Susan "Sue" Hester,
who offered me love, laughter,
great food, and a lot of wisdom.

CONTENTS

FOREWORD

When Billy Hester asked me to write the foreword for this book, I was surprised and a little flattered. You see, I'm not a famous writer, nor have I ever had any of my writings honored officially — except for a book review I wrote in the seventh grade a long, long time ago. As a prize, I got a hardcover copy of *The Winston Senior Dictionary*, which I still have after sixty years. I also have my handwritten submission, written in cursive on lined paper, believe it or not!

My credentials for this task mainly derive from the fact that I have sat in the Asbury Memorial sanctuary on Sunday mornings for a little less than ten years. I already have experienced many of the stories in this book, delivered as part of one of Billy's sermons.

As you read this book, I encourage you to imagine that you are sitting in the pews too.

Before the service begins, you would experience the joy and fellowship of greeting your fellow congregants with hugs and laughter — they alone make attendance worthwhile. Then, you would follow the order of worship leading up to the sermon, which almost always would get you into a place to receive its wisdom. As you listened to Billy deliver the sermon, you likely would feel uplifted. Sometimes, your eyes would moisten as you tried to keep from sobbing with joy. The lovely stained-glass windows, with sunlight that changes with the time of year filtering through, would help to set your mood.

So, what's the bottom line? By experiencing Billy Hester's sermon stories first-hand, I have received wisdom for my life. I have sensed the unlimited love that God has for everyone, including you and me. It has been a wonderful journey. I also have grown to be more loving to everyone I encounter along the way. I've learned that Jesus excluded no one, and neither should those who profess to be His followers.

The stories in this book reflect real events in Billy's life that he has shared with his congregation, both in sermons from the pulpit and in the everyday life of our fellowship as a cell in the Body of Christ. I am glad to help him share them with you, the reader.

While you are reading the book—or after you've finished it—I encourage you to contemplate the questions at the end of each story. If you have several kindred spirits, ask them to join you in a study group. I fully expect that everyone in the group will receive blessings by doing so.

Also, if you haven't read Billy's first book, *Wow! Moments*, do yourself a favor and read it. You will learn about Billy's path to his ministry, his growth in the Spirit, and his positive impact at Asbury Memorial.

Frank D. Ramsey
Longtime congregant of Asbury Memorial
Editor of this book and Billy's first book, *Wow! Moments*
Savannah, Georgia, 2018

ACKNOWLEDGMENTS

First of all, I thank Dr. Choon-Leong Seow. In 1988, he taught my first course about wisdom literature at Princeton Theological Seminary, introducing me to the wealth of wisdom writings in the sacred texts. I continue to discover nuggets there!

Thanks also to the members of my Asbury Memorial congregation who helped proofread (and cheerlead) this book: Wayne Bland, Susan Bolinger, Iris Dayoub, Melissa Gratias, Cheri Hester, Ginger Miles, Grady Mills, Barry Parker, and Kate Strain. They all have helped make this book better, and I am grateful for their help.

I especially thank the book's illustrator, Mimi Mangrum Numer, for her clever spot illustrations that make the book more interesting. After you've read a story, go back to the illustration; you'll better understand its imagery.

And, of course, I thank my chief go-to person, Frank Ramsey, for helping me edit and publish this book. Thanks also to Danny Lewis, his spouse, for letting me invade their home during work sessions.

❦

Finally, I thank my family and friends for their love and support and for the wisdom imparted during our times together.

Introduction

One of my favorite classes at Princeton Theological Seminary was called "Israel's Wisdom Literature." The course focused on the books of Proverbs, Job, and Ecclesiastes, along with other material in the Bible that scholars classify as wisdom writings.

The course did not get off to a good start for me. My professor kept talking about some guy named "Kohelet." "Kohelet this," and "Kohelet that." Everyone seemed to know who the professor was talking about except me. My classmates even asked questions about Kohelet. I kept checking the description of the course: "Israel's Wisdom Literature: Proverbs, Job, and Ecclesiastes." I didn't see anything about a Kohelet.

Being the only one in the class who didn't have a clue about Kohelet, I was too embarrassed to ask anyone who he was. Since Kohelet wasn't in the course's description, I figured that he wasn't too important and that everyone would soon stop talking about him. They didn't.

My best friend in seminary was an Oklahoman named Rodney Newman, who I thought could help me. Rodney wasn't in the class, but he was a biblical genius. He most likely would know who Kohelet was. Since Rodney already knew how unlearned I was, I felt comfortable asking him. He

4

smiled and said, "Billy, that's who wrote the book of Ecclesiastes. It's just another way of saying Ecclesiastes."

I opened the Bible to Ecclesiastes 1:1, and sure enough, the name Kohelet was in the footnotes. In my defense, most English translations use the word "Teacher" or "Preacher." To make it even more mysterious, "Qoheleth" is another way of spelling Kohelet.

This revelation was not good news. Since I didn't think Kohelet was important, I hadn't taken down any notes about him. In other words, I did not have any notes about the book of Ecclesiastes.

Somehow, I still ended up doing well in the class, probably because I loved the subject. It was fascinating to discover that there is a substantial portion of the Bible that is similar to teachings in Eastern religions. Who knew that wisdom is a large part of the Judeo-Christian tradition? Often, we think of religion as spiritual, mysterious, and ethereal. And indeed, it is those things. But it is more. A large part of most major religions has to do with something hands-on and practical: knowledge gained from our experiences. Wisdom is what we learn from our experiences or the experiences of others, which can help us greatly in our daily living. For instance, after having my experience about Kohelet, I never again hesitated to ask my seminary professors any questions.

Having wisdom is different from being smart. If I asked you to close your eyes and think of someone who is *smart*, my hunch is that you would think of someone from the age of eighteen to forty. If I asked you to close your eyes and think of someone who is *wise*, my hunch is that you would picture someone who is over fifty. The longer we live, and the more experiences we have, the more opportunities we have to gain wisdom. But in order to achieve this, we need to be observant and to be open to learning.

This book shares some of the experiences that have been great teaching moments in my life. In a sense, *Wow! Wisdom* is just the opposite of my first book, *Wow! Moments*, which focused on synchronicities that tend to be rare and unique. *Wow! Wisdom* focuses on what we can learn from the common experiences we have in our daily lives. As my old friend, Chris Wilburn, used to say, "Billy creates a sermon from a trip to the grocery store."

In a handful of the stories, I highlight some of the sage advice that the stories seem to offer. On other occasions, I simply share the story and leave it to the readers to decide what pearls of wisdom they can squeeze from it.

Wisdom challenges us to ask questions, to reason, to think. Wisdom acknowledges that it has limitations—that God is God and there are mysteries that humanity cannot understand. But wisdom also believes that a person can influence his or her destiny—that our knowledge and decisions can affect the future. Wisdom teaches that, if a person doesn't question and search for truth, he or she is not fulfilling their responsibility as a human being.

❧

The word "path" is a universal term in wisdom traditions. The writers of the books in the Bible mentioned a path many, many times, especially in Proverbs and Psalms. For example: "I have taught you the way of wisdom; I have led you in the paths of uprightness" (Proverbs 4:11) and "You show me the path of life. In your presence there is fullness of joy; in your right hand are pleasures forevermore" (Psalm 16:11).

When I hear the word "path," I think immediately of Bluffton, South Carolina. One of my grandmothers lived there, right on the May River—fishing dock and all. The best place to swim was a swimming hole about a hundred yards from her house. To get to it, we walked barefoot down a well-worn, winding path. It was a beautiful stroll on the bluff along the river among the pine trees.

Oh yes, those pine trees! The squirrels would get in the trees, pick off a pine cone, and chew on it so the sharp leaves of the cone would fall off and cover the path below. In order to get to the great swimming hole, people had to walk along a path that was covered with bits and pieces of pine cones. When I stepped on them, they hurt—*really* hurt!

What was even more distressing was that no one else seemed bothered by them. Instead of tiptoeing and walking slowly, my cousins walked quickly—sometimes they even ran down the path. I wondered, "What were their feet made of?"

I didn't let on about how painful it was for me. Whenever I walked with someone on the path, I gritted my teeth, smiled, and pretended that I was pain-free. If the person decided to run on ahead and encouraged me to run with them, I'd say, "No, I just want to enjoy this lovely stroll through the woods." Then, when I was alone, I'd let my feelings out and start hopping all over the place.

One time I invited a girlfriend over to Bluffton. As we started to walk the path, I was going to show her how tough I was. I knew that when she realized there were obstacles on the path, she would need help. I would let her slow down and would comfort her. Maybe I would even pick her up and carry her down to the swimming hole. But the pine cone pieces didn't seem to bother her either. In fact, she ended up beating me down to the swimming hole too!

I still remember the day I was walking down the path with one of my cousins, a cousin I had walked down the path with countless times, a cousin who always had walked down the path with ease. But on this occasion, he took a step and said, "OUCH! These pine cones can really hurt sometimes!"

"They sure can," I said. I couldn't believe that he actually was injured. I couldn't believe that he acknowledged the pain. I was sorry that my cousin was hurt, but, at the same time, it felt good not to be alone in my pain.

Like the path in Bluffton, life is beautiful but also painful—it can really hurt. I hope this book reminds you that you are not alone in celebrating the joys in life and acknowledging the hurts, as you seek to gain wisdom on the path of life.

Blessings and Peace,
Billy "Kohelet" Hester

USING THE STORY QUESTIONS

Following each of the stories, I have suggested questions for readers to use as springboards for personal reflection or for group discussions. Since we all gain wisdom from our experiences, the questions ultimately should have us ask, "What lessons are in the story? What wisdom do we gain?" If you are reading the book on your own, you may find the questions helpful for prayer and reflection when you read or revisit a story. If you use the questions in a group setting, enlist a facilitator to establish ground rules for the discussion. Here are some ideas for group members:

- Be an active and attentive listener.
- Encourage only one person to speak at a time.
- Speak from personal experience, using "I" statements without generalizing.
- Allow space for others to share, while being sensitive to the amount of time that you share.
- Avoid trying to fix someone or solve their problems.
- Agree that it's okay to disagree—another person's experience may introduce you to a totally different perspective on the matter that may be helpful for you.
- Last but not least, keep confidentiality.

Marriage Vows
with the "Hells Angels"

I n the early 1990s, I was asked by a woman named
Rebecca Herdman to officiate a citywide renewal-of-
vows ceremony for married couples. Rebecca worked
for City Market, a quaint historic area in downtown
Savannah, Georgia, filled with restaurants and shops. She
thought it would be cool to offer a renewal-of-vows
ceremony at City Market on Valentine's Day.

When I worked at Marble Collegiate Church in New York
City, I participated in a renewal-of-vows ceremony; and it
was very meaningful for the participants. I agreed with
Rebecca that it was worth a try.

On the day of the event, I drove downtown, parked my
car, and walked to City Market with my black clerical robe in
hand. As I turned the corner to go down the main street, I was
surprised at what I saw: motorcycle after motorcycle after
motorcycle. Every motorcycle in the state of Georgia was
parked in front of a bar called "Malone's."

I had seen groups of motorcyclists before, but nothing like
this. It looked like a Hells Angels convention! The dress of the

collection of bikers matched my stereotypes: bandanas, beards, chains, leather, spikes, boots, jeans, tattoos, and vests. It felt like I had walked onto the set of a *Mad Max* movie. My first thought was, "Oh no! What have I gotten myself into?"

I had been told that the platform I was to stand on while leading the ceremony was set up in front of Malone's. "Let me get this straight," I thought. "I'm to lead a serious and meaningful ceremony for couples to renew their marriage vows right in front of a hundred drunk and rowdy motorcyclists who are having the time of their lives at an indoor/outdoor bar? Who wants to ask them to be quiet? Who wants to tell them their party is over? Who wants to die?"

I could imagine the noise the bikers would be making— all the shouting and hellraising (no pun intended). They will heckle and tease the participants. "This is a big mistake," I thought. "This is going to be a disaster." But it was too late to back out. I would just have to grin and bear it. "Just do it, Billy. Get it over and never agree to do it again."

An announcement came over the PA system that it was time for the ceremony to begin. What happened next took my anxiety to an even higher level. All of the Hells Angels got up from their seats at Malone's and came over to the area where we were to have the ceremony. They weren't just planning to watch it—they were planning to be part of it! It was bad enough for the bikers to be loud and obnoxious at the bar off to the side. But now they would be right in the middle of things. They would be in front of me, and they would be interspersed with "non-biker" couples. It would be impossible to ignore their outbursts.

After taking a few deep breaths, I made my introductory

remarks to the crowd. I shared that the vows they were about to make were not any less important than the vows they first made on their wedding day. "In fact," I said, "they are even more significant. On the day you got married, you didn't know what it meant to love the person standing beside you in sickness and in health, in prosperity and in need, in joy and in sorrow. You didn't know what it meant to be committed to this person forever. Now you know what it means to be committed to each other through the ups and downs, the high and lows of a marriage. Today, we celebrate your marriage and your commitment."

As the couples faced each other and held hands, I led them in an exchange of vows. There were no outbursts; there was no heckling; there were no jokes. You could hear a pin drop. The only sounds that came from the bikers were the words of commitment they said to their spouses—and the sniffles that accompanied them. I was stunned.

After the ceremony, a biker-gal came up to me with tears in her eyes and mascara running down her cheeks. "That was wonderful!" she said. "It meant so much to me." Holding a big black book, she held it out to me and said, "Would you please sign my Bible? I always want to remember this day." The woman was *actually* carrying a Bible. It was the first and only time someone asked me to sign their Bible.

After hanging out for a while with my new biker friends, I walked back to my car with my robe in hand and my tail between my legs. When will I ever learn not to judge people?

❧

It's been about twenty-five years since that day, and we still do a renewal of marriage vows every evening on

Valentine's Day at City Market. After the first couple of years officiating the ceremony solo, I got smart and asked my wife, Cheri, to join me in leading it. That way, we can be with each other on Valentine's Day, and we can renew our vows too.

Another bonus has to do with City Market and my family history. About fifteen years ago, the folks at City Market asked Cheri and me to stand in a gazebo to lead the ceremony. The gazebo happens to be on the corner of Congress and Jefferson Streets—which is right in front of the building that housed my father's restaurant, called "Hester's."

It had been a bar owned by my grandfather in the 1950s, but my father transformed it into one of the finest eating establishments in the city. My father died in 1963 when I was four years old, so I didn't get to know him or experience his restaurant. But each year on February 14th, I have a special connection with my father and the neighborhood where he spent so much of his time.

If you are married and if you ever find yourself in or near Savannah on February 14th, come on down to City Market and join us. The Hesters would love to see you in front of where the old Hester's used to be. We may not have as many bikers at the ceremony as we did that first year, but we will have a whole lot of other people. All kinds of people! My biker friends taught me that everyone should be welcomed.

STUDY QUESTIONS

- Have you ever prejudged someone and ended up being wrong about the person? What was the situation?

- What are some consequences of stereotyping?

- What can help us grow out of a judgmental attitude?

- In the Renewal-of-Vows Service, Billy often will mention this quote by Dietrich Bonhoeffer, "It is not your love that sustains the marriage, but, from now on, the marriage that sustains your love." Do you agree with Bonhoeffer? What does his quote mean to you?

- Billy mentions that vows in a renewal-of-vows ceremony can be just as significant as, if not more significant than, the vows a couple took on their wedding day. How can that be?

- Have you ever been in a situation that you thought was going to be horrible but turned out to be one of the best experiences in your life? What did you learn from it?

- What will you remember most from this story?

UNCLE PHIL AND THE BLIND MAN

O ne of the three persons to whom I dedicated my first book was the late Phillip Harris Hunter Sr., better known as "Uncle Phil." He was one of those larger-than-life characters that people never forget. I once had a very successful actor friend tell me, "If you could get your Uncle Phil to move to New York, he would make a mint doing commercials."

When Uncle Phil was a young man in the early 1950s, he wasn't sure what to do with his life. He decided to go to a career counselor to take a test that would suggest occupations that would be a good fit for him. The results of the test came back, declaring that he should either be a preacher or a salesman. Phil told the man who gave him the test, "Since I don't feel the callin', I guess I better be a salesman." So that's what he did.

Phil ended up working for Liggett and Myers Tobacco Company. It wasn't long before the corporate leaders realized they had a jewel of a salesman in Phil Hunter. He traveled the world for the company. He was so good at his craft, the company used him to train other salesmen. But what Phil Hunter had is something you can't teach. It was a unique gift he was born with: connecting and communicating with people.

Liggett and Myers had their offices in Raleigh-Durham, North Carolina, but Phil's wife, my Aunt Bette, did not want to move and leave her hometown of Savannah. The corporate leaders wanted Uncle Phil so badly that they allowed him to live in Savannah, and they flew him to his office every week in North Carolina. As a child, I didn't realize that this was unusual. The older I got, and the more time I spent with Uncle Phil, the more I realized how unique this man was.

After I moved to New York, Uncle Phil was the family member I would see most frequently because he would come to New York on business. He would let me stay with him at the Essex House, one of the best hotels in Manhattan. It was fun to see Uncle Phil performing his magic with people in the big city.

For much of my life, I had seen Uncle Phil as a storyteller and a fun person to be with, but someone you took with a grain of salt. After all, he was full of "fish tales." As I matured, I discovered that many of his exaggerations were clever metaphors—kernels of truth wrapped in stories and one-liners. I came to realize that much of his advice was coming from someone who had seen the world, someone who had had many great experiences, and someone who had gained much wisdom.

When I started attending Marble Collegiate Church in New York City, I had the opportunity to hear Dr. Norman Vincent Peale preach every Sunday. He was known as one of the great orators and storytellers of the 20th century. His manner of speaking and storytelling reminded me so much of Uncle Phil and the way he communicated. Besides being a great storyteller, Uncle Phil had a great understanding of people and human nature. The career counselor was right — Phil Hunter would have made an incredible preacher and minister.

In 1973, while Uncle Phil was still flying to and from work in Raleigh-Durham, he and my Aunt Bette decided to open a shop in Savannah. It would be a combination lamp and tobacco shop. Their teenage daughter and son, Kim and Phil Jr., helped with the business. They would work at the shop when they weren't in school.

When I was fourteen, Aunt Bette and Uncle Phil would let me join my cousins working at Ye Ole Tobacco Shop and Verdery's on Saturdays. They were helping me learn a trade and helping me build my self-esteem. Or, as Uncle Phil would say, he was teaching my cousins and me how to keep our hands out of our pockets!

On one of those Saturdays, a blind man entered the shop. He wore dark glasses and was led by a seeing-eye dog. When Uncle Phil noticed the man, he raised his index finger in the air and quietly said to my cousins and me in his rich baritone voice, "I'll take this one."

The blind man quietly stepped up to the counter and said that he was interested in buying a pipe. These were really nice pipes—expensive—so if you could get someone to buy a pipe, you had made the sale of the day.

"Yes, sir," my Uncle Phil said. "You've come to the right place. We can help you with that."

Uncle Phil pulled out three or four pipes and put them on the glass counter and said, "Don't these look lovely? (He actually said, "Don't these look lovely?" to a blind man!) Rubbing more salt into the wound, he added, "Have you ever seen anything so beautiful in your life?"

My cousins and I couldn't believe it. Our jaws dropped as Uncle Phil kept putting his foot in his mouth time and time again with his "visual comments." We didn't know whether to laugh or cry. On one hand, it seemed like a skit from *Saturday Night Live*. On the other hand, we were afraid the man's feelings would be hurt and that he might get angry.

Uncle Phil continued the conversation, "Partner, aren't these magnificent?"

Then the man and Uncle Phil started feeling the pipes together—all four hands were on one of the pipes. It looked like they were playing a piano duet on a keyboard. Uncle Phil continued with comments like, "This one is marvelous! Makes you look like a million dollars!" This crazy scene and discussion went on for about twenty minutes.

After the lovefest between my uncle and the blind man was over, the sale was complete. The man ended up buying three pipes, six lighters, and eighty pounds of tobacco! The man walked out of the store on Cloud Nine, wishing everyone a great day!

My cousins and I were stunned. We couldn't believe what we had just witnessed. How did Uncle Phil get away with that? And how did he get the man to buy so much?

After Uncle Phil said his final goodbyes to the man, he moseyed over to us and quietly said, "The man just wants to be treated like everyone else."

Was this good salesmanship or good religion? Or both?

Everyone may be different, but Uncle Phil knew that we all have the same basic needs and desires. Everyone wants to be known; everyone wants to be loved; everyone wants and needs to be lifted up.

Uncle Phil didn't have to choose between being a salesman or a minister after all. He ended up being both.

STUDY QUESTIONS

- If you've been to a career counselor, what occupation(s) did they suggest for you to pursue?

- If you've never been to a career counselor, what occupation(s) do you think a career counselor would suggest for you to pursue?

- Why did Phil want his salespersons to keep their hands out of their pockets? What was he trying to teach?

- Why do you think Phil wanted to be the salesperson for the blind man?

- Why do you think Phil was so successful with his sale?

- What was Phil implying when he said, "The man just wants to be treated like everyone else?"

- What will you remember most from this story?

THE MIRACLE AT BACON PARK

From age six to eleven, I played football for the Bacon Park Eagles. We had quite a team. Every year, we went undefeated. No one even scored on us. Many of the players went on to star on high school and college teams. One of our teammates was Gary Lanier, who played quarterback at Georgia Tech during the years that the colorful Pepper Rodgers coached the team. Another one of our players, Steve Kelly, was on the University of Georgia's 1980 National Championship Team with Herschel Walker. In fact, Steve and his brother, Bob, happened to make a critical play together that helped win the championship game.

But for me, playing football was not just about winning or losing. Since my father died when I was four and since I didn't have brothers, it was essential for me to have male role models and male companionship. My coaches and teammates played an important role in my emotional and psychological development. Playing football also strengthened my confidence and buoyed my self-esteem.

Every year, however, there was a concern that I would not have the opportunity to play football. Before the start of each season, every boy who wanted to be on a team had to be weighed at what we called the "weigh-in." In order to be on a city football team, you could not weigh over a certain amount. They didn't want the very heavy boys tackling or falling on the very small boys. Every boy in our area had to go to the Farmers Market in Garden City, Georgia, for the weigh-in. This was an incredibly stressful time for me because I was big for my age. I was what we called "husky."

Most of the time, being husky was not a positive attribute. Going shopping for clothes was torture. Every time my mother and I would go into a department store, the salesman would look at me and say, "Ma'am, you're not going to find anything for him in this section. You're going to have to take him over to the husky section."

The one good thing about being husky is that everyone wanted me to play on their football team. The question was: Would I be able to play; would I be under the weight limit?

Every year I'd sweat it out. Before each season started, I'd try to lose weight. Fortunately, I always would be just barely under the maximum amount. I would be so relieved. If you passed the weigh-in, then you were home free for the rest of the season. I could relax and focus on playing ball.

In 1969, when I was ten years old, something happened during the middle of the football season that had never happened before. We were about to play a team at Bacon Park Field on a Saturday morning. Just before the game was about to start, the coach from the other team started walking across the field. When he arrived on our side, he went over to our coach, Donald West, and spoke to him. Then Coach West pointed to me and said, "Billy, they want to weigh you."

The Miracle at Bacon Park

They want to do what? They never weigh players after the season starts! They can't weigh me! I had gone back to my old eating habits. The weight limit for me that year was 115 pounds, and I knew I had exceeded it. I was in big trouble!

The other team's coach, Coach West, and I walked across the field to the parking lot—I was filled with anxiety. He led us to his car, opened his trunk, and pulled out a bathroom scale—he actually brought a bathroom scale to the game. "Are you kidding me?" I thought. He put it on the ground. Knowing that I was over the weight limit but knowing that my football pads would make me way over the limit, I started stripping. The helmet flew off, the shoulder pads, the cleats, the pads that were inside my pants—I got down to as light as I could possibly be.

Standing practically naked in a parking lot before a Saturday morning game, I stepped on the scale. Bathroom scales were not digital back in those days. This was a traditional scale with the red meter line in front of a numerical background. The meter line quickly shot forward. It reached its pinnacle. Then it started wobbling back and forth, back and forth, until it finally stopped. I could not believe my eyes. It landed right on the number 115!

After letting out a great sigh of relief, I hopped off the scale, threw on all my gear, and sprinted across the field to my teammates as fast as my little, husky legs could take me! I could play! I could play! I could be part of the team! I could be an Eagle!

❧

In one of his sermons, homiletics professor Fred Craddock said, "One of the most beautiful words in the

English language is the word *included*. And one of the ugliest words is the word *excluded*."

We all have things that can make us feel different or odd, things that make us feel like an outsider. For me, it was being husky and not having a father. For other people, it could be the color of their skin, their nationality, their sexual orientation, their economic status, their gender, their age, or their addictions, among many other things. Everybody has something that makes her or him feel "less than." I didn't realize it back then, but I'm sure that even the coach who pulled out the bathroom scale from his trunk had stuff that made him feel like an outsider too.

I've often wondered what would have happened had my weight gone over the limit that day. How embarrassed would I have been? Would I have gone home? Or would I have stood on the sideline in humiliation watching my teammates play?

I don't know. But I am thankful for the miracle at Bacon Park. Not just because I could play and be part of the team, but because it has made me more sensitive to other people who may not feel included.

STUDY QUESTIONS

- What things about yourself make you feel odd or different?

- Do you ever feel excluded? If so, how?

- If you had been Billy, and you had been over the weight limit, and you could not play in the game, how would you have reacted? Would you have gone home? Would you have stayed and watched the game? Or something else?

- Who are your teammates? How do they make you feel included?

- What are things you do that may make people feel excluded?

- What are things you can do to be more sensitive to including others?

- What will you remember most from this story?

PLAYING YOUR OWN MUSIC

My wife and I love to dance!
Our families love to dance!!
Our friends love to dance!!!

When Cheri and I were planning our wedding, we decided that the one thing we wanted to invest in was a band. We wanted to supply a good jazz band, so everyone could have a wonderful time dancing at the reception.

Cheri and I were living in New York at the time and planning our wedding there. Since we had careers in the arts, you would think we would know something about bands. But we had been in the world of theatre. We knew actors, singers, dancers, choreographers, directors—not bands. The world of bands was foreign to us.

Cheri got a phone book, looked up bands, and called some of them. One was the Stan Rubin Band. Cheri spoke with Mr. Rubin and asked if he had a tape of his band, so we could listen to a sample of their music. He said, "No, I can't help you there. But we are playing for a big gala at the Museum of Natural History this Friday. Why don't you dress up and crash the party? That way you can hear what we sound like."

So that's what we did. We put on formal attire and went to the event at the Museum of Natural History to hear the band. As Cheri and I walked toward a huge room, we could hear wonderful music. When we got closer, we could see a large orchestra: violins, trumpets, trombones, french horns—you name it. They had a thirty-piece band playing between the legs of huge dinosaurs. The band sounded like Tommy Dorsey's or Benny Goodman's bands—just tremendous!

We, of course, couldn't afford to hire that many musicians. But Stan explained, "What I'll do is pick five of my best musicians out of the orchestra to form the band." That sounded good to us. How could we go wrong? They were incredible! Top notch!

We got married. We left the big Fifth Avenue church to go to the Princeton Club for the reception. (One of the perks of attending Princeton Theological Seminary was the opportunity to have the reception at the Princeton Club in Manhattan.)

Now it was time for the bride and groom's first dance. Cheri and I walked to the center of the dance floor for the big moment. The band started playing, and it was hard to describe the sound we heard. It was awful!

The trumpet was especially off. With the trumpet's loud and dominating sound, it was very important to have an excellent trumpet player. We apparently didn't have one. The squeaking and the off-pitch sounds were piercing.

I looked over at the band to see who was playing the trumpet. I almost fainted. The guy looked to be 110 years old! He was bone thin and wearing a black toupee that looked perfect for a thirty-year-old. He looked as though he could not muster up enough air to blow a feather, much less a trumpet.

Cheri and I faced each other for our dance. I'll never forget the look on her face; she looked like a deer caught in the headlights. I pulled her close to me for our dance and whispered in her ear, "What are we going to do?"

"I don't know," she said, "this is terrible."

People had flown from Georgia, Maryland, Chicago, and other parts of the known world for the wedding. We had our New York friends there who were performers and knew good music. We had come together to celebrate and to dance, but we had a lousy band.

Besides being disappointed and embarrassed, I was also angry. Apparently, they had pulled a fast one on us. They thought they could get away with giving these two young people their second-string musicians. And we fell for it. We had been taken.

After Cheri and I danced, it was time for the bride's dance with her father. As Cheri and her father danced, we suffered through another squeaky rendition of a song we had requested.

When that song mercifully ended, the emcee said, "Now everyone is invited onto the dance floor!" "This is going to be horrible," I thought. "No one will want to dance." To the credit of our family and friends, they rushed out onto the dance floor. I was so thankful that they didn't let the band's music hinder their enthusiasm. What wonderful friends we had!

The couple dancing right next to Cheri and me was Karl

Jurman and Mary D'Arcy. We had known Karl and Mary since our very first days of living in New York. Mary and Cheri had been in the musical *Singin' in the Rain* on Broadway. Mary played Kathy Selden, the lead role Debbie Reynolds made famous in the film.

But I knew Karl and Mary even before Cheri did. In 1981, I had been in an original show which Karl had written the music for, and he was the show's musical director. Karl went on to be a musical director and conductor for *The Lion King* on Broadway. These two people were expert musicians. I didn't even want to imagine what they thought about our band.

I looked over at them, and Karl had the biggest smile I've ever seen on a person's face. I assumed that Karl couldn't contain himself—must be laughing at our crazy band. As he is smiling and dancing, he shouts to me over the music, "Billy, this is great!"

I shouted back, "It is?"

He said, "How did you do it?"

I said, "Do what?"

"How did you get Doc Cheatham to play for your reception?"

I said, "What?"

"How did you get Doc Cheatham to play for your reception?"

"What do you mean?"

Karl gestured to the band as he danced and said, "How did you get the legendary trumpeter to play for you?"

I looked over at the skinny, 110-year-old man, and then looked back at Karl and said, "Oh, him?" trying not to look surprised. "Well, we've got our ways!"

Apparently, the 110-year-old man was a big deal! Apparently, he was a legend!

All of a sudden, the music started sounding good— *reeeally* good. The trumpet's notes became pure and sweet. The toupee still looked a bit odd, but the music was heavenly! The band played masterfully the rest of the night, and everyone had a wonderful time!

It dawned on me what had happened. The first two songs the band played were songs Cheri and I had requested. They were songs we chose for our first dance and for Cheri's dance with her father. They were not the band's songs. For our two songs, the band needed sheet music. They were reading the notes as they tried to play our requested songs.

After the band played our songs, they started playing their music in the style they preferred. They didn't need sheet music for their songs. In fact, the sheet music inhibited them. Doc and the other musicians needed to feel the music. And they did. We witnessed a transformation. They went from being awful to being awesome!

The rest of the night, I went around telling people at the reception that we were blessed to have Doc Cheatham—the Legend—the Babe Ruth of Jazz—playing for us!

Eight years later, on a quiet night in 1995, Cheri and I were in bed watching *The Tonight Show*. After one or two guest interviews, the host, Jay Leno, said, "And now we've got a special treat. Here tonight, celebrating his ninetieth birthday and playing for us, is the legendary Doc Cheatham!"

And Doc came out and played his trumpet. Later that night, Ted Koppel interviewed Doc on *Nightline*. Karl was right! We did have a legend playing for us.

They were not honoring Doc on television because he was a jazz legend who turned ninety. They were honoring him because he was a ninety-year-old jazz legend who was playing just as many gigs now as he did when he was a young man. In fact, Doc agreed with the critical assessment that he was probably the only jazz musician to create his best work after the age of seventy.

Doc would make his transition two years later in 1997. He had just recorded an album and had played a full set at a jazz club in Georgetown two days before he died. That's amazing! Talk about going out in style!

Thank you, Doc, for playing at our reception. Forgive me for taking a while to discover what a blessing you were. I look forward to hearing your horn again one day!

STUDY QUESTIONS

- Do you like to dance? How does dancing make you feel?

- If you had been Billy, what would you have said to Cheri during your first dance, when you both realized how bad the band sounded?

- Metaphorically, do you prefer to live your life reading sheet music, or do you prefer to live without the music in front of you? How do you play best? Why?

- What lessons can we learn from the way Doc Cheatham lived his life?

- What would you like to be doing when you are ninety years old?

- What do you suppose would have happened had Karl not told Billy who the trumpet player was?

- What will you remember most from this story?

ABSOLUTELY AMAZING

I n the 1990s, a group from my church annually attended a weeklong Music & Arts Conference at Lake Junaluska, North Carolina. Lake Junaluska is a beautiful United Methodist conference center, nestled in the Smoky Mountains about thirty miles west of Asheville.

The first year we attended the Music & Arts Week, Cheri and I didn't realize how popular it was and how well-attended it would be. When we went to rent a cabin for our family, we were surprised to discover that all the cabins had been booked. We'd have to find a place off-campus.

We finally found a house about twenty minutes from Junaluska. Many of the houses and cottages in that part of North Carolina are given names. For instance, some of the names of the homes in that area were Robin's Nest, Cozy Cottage, Bee Hive, and Butterfly House. The name of the house we rented was "Absolutely Amazing." That sounded like a winner to me!

We drove to North Carolina and picked up the key for the house at a rental office. The manager pointed in the direction of a huge mountain and said, "It's on top of that big mountain."

So, we started driving up the mountain. At first, it was like regular mountain roads and curves. But as we got higher, the terrain got more and more primitive. We saw only a few houses along the way. The more we kept going up, the more undeveloped it was. Before long, there were no houses in sight.

What we started seeing were mirrors that had been embedded into the bark of trees. Why had mirrors been attached to trees? We soon realized that, without the mirrors, you could not see what was coming around the corners of the narrow paths we were driving on. The mirrors at least gave you an idea of what you would be crashing into around the next bend.

By now, we were very high on the mountain. All of a sudden, the car started pointing up—straight up. You know, when you're on a roller coaster and it's about to climb that last, big peak for the last, big plunge, and your cart turns straight up towards the sky, putting all the force of gravity on your back? That's what we experienced in the car. Packed with Cheri, four children, Grandma, and me, the strained car slowly moved up and up. The kids started screaming. I was screaming. I didn't think it was the right time to let them know that I wasn't a very good mountain driver. It was then that I realized why they called this house "Absolutely Amazing." It is *absolutely amazing* if you survive the ride to the house!

Well, we did. We finally got there, and the house was great. It lived up to its name, for the view from the top of that mountain was indeed absolutely amazing.

The next morning, we went back down the mountain to the conference at Junaluska. Cheri and the kids were all participating in workshops. I, on the other hand, was just there to take it easy and enjoy the scenery. Church member Chris Wilburn had brought his daughter, Jennie, to the workshop, so Chris also had some free time. He and I decided that we would make ourselves useful and make sandwiches for our church members for lunch.

I said, "Hey, Chris, why don't we go to my place to make the sandwiches. I want you to see it. It's got a great view. C'mon and ride with me." I wanted to surprise him with our special roller coaster ride to the top. I couldn't wait to hear Chris shriek—which he did.

When we arrived, I gave him a tour of the house. Then we went to the kitchen and started making sandwiches. All of a sudden, we heard what sounded like a knock on the door. Chris and I looked at each other. We knew that nobody could be up where we were, so we ignored the sound and went back to our peanut butter and jelly. Then we heard the sound again. There *was* someone at the door! Who could it be? Who would climb all the way to the top of this isolated mountain? Who would ride on those narrow, treacherous paths with mirrors embedded into the trees? Who would point their car skyward as if they were on the Scream Machine?

Chris went to the front door to see who it was. I stayed in the kitchen. I don't know why I didn't follow him. It could have been dangerous—Chris opening the door to strangers all alone on top of a mountain. I had seen *Deliverance*! I know what dueling banjos sound like!

Chris opened the door, and someone apparently said something to him, because Chris responded by saying, "Oh. Hi!"

Then he yelled back to me in his loudest voice: "Hey Billy! It's the Jehovah's Witnesses!"

The Jehovah's Witnesses? Are you kidding me? Unbelievable! Talk about commitment! These people climbed Mount Everest just to come knock on our door.

Now I *knew* I didn't want to go to the door. The last thing I wanted to do on my vacation was get into a theological debate with Jehovah's Witnesses. The last thing I wanted to do was deal with people. So, I continued to hide in the kitchen.

Now you had to know Chris Wilburn to really appreciate this story. Chris was an extreme extrovert. He loved to be with people, and he had an incredible sense of humor.

The next thing he said to the Jehovah's Witnesses was, "How did you find us? We came all the way up here to get away from you people!"

Fortunately, one of the Jehovah's Witnesses also had a sense of humor. He said in a deep, bass voice, "You can run, but you can't hide!"

Chris laughed. The Jehovah's Witnesses laughed. I stayed in the kitchen.

About twenty minutes later, Chris came back to the kitchen with a great big smile on his face. "They were interesting people. I really enjoyed talking with them." I was amazed. I found Chris' way with people "absolutely amazing."

❧

Absolutely Amazing

Maybe one reason Chris was such a good people person was because he was isolated for a long time as a child. When the cases of polio surged in our country in the early 1950s, Chris was one of its last victims, just missing Jonas Salk's important polio vaccine that came out in 1955. The isolation Chris endured in an iron lung, the isolation for so long in a bed, the isolation for so long in his room created a human being that understood the sacred gift of fellowship and being with others. Polio left Chris without the use of one of his arms, but it also left him with an adventurous spirit, a great love for people, and a keen sense of humor.

His sudden death from a heart attack on May 18, 2008, stunned us all. But he didn't leave us before touching many, many lives.

May the Spirit of Chris Wilburn continue to inspire us.

May the Spirit of Chris help us to reach out to strangers.

May the Spirit of Chris help us to get out of the kitchen.

STUDY QUESTIONS

- Where do you go to get away from it all?

- What places are "thin places" for you—places where you sense the holy or the greatness and presence of God? Are they places of beauty, majesty, quietness—or something else?

- The mirrors on the road to Absolutely Amazing helped drivers see what was coming around the curves. What "mirrors" do you have in your life to help you make decisions? Who are your mirrors that point out potential danger spots?

- Chris Wilburn's experience with polio as a child helped him develop an appreciation for being with people. Have you had a negative experience in your life that helped you develop or discover a strength? What was it?

- Needing to get "out of the kitchen" can be a metaphor for many things. What does it mean for you? What do you need to work on? What area of growth?

- If you need to get "out of the kitchen" in an area of your life, what can help you achieve this goal? What resources are there for you?

- What will you remember most from this story?

MARIA'S MERCEDES

etween my junior and senior years of college, I had
the pleasure of being in a theatrical company in
Vermont. It was the summer of 1980 and the first time
I had spent time away from South Georgia. A summer in
Vermont was a magnificent way to be introduced to another
part of the United States. A winter in Vermont would be
challenging for me, but June through August was heavenly.
Every night, I could hear Willie Nelson singing "Moonlight
in Vermont."

The summer stock company I was part of was a training
ground for young actors called "Green Mountain Guild."
Some of its alumni included Meryl Streep and Timothy
Busfield. The shows we performed that summer were the
musicals *Oliver* and *My Fair Lady*. We took our productions
to four different areas of Vermont: Quechee, Killington,
Mount Snow, and Stowe.

Quechee is known for its old, covered bridges; Killington
for its ski resorts; Mount Snow for its snowboarding and
Winter X Games; and Stowe for a well-known family home,
the Trapp Family Lodge. Yes, Stowe, Vermont, is where

Maria von Trapp and the Baron decided to settle down in the United States. They left Austria in 1938 to tour as the Trapp Family Singers. In the early 1940s, the family bought a farm in Stowe. They built a beautiful mountain home on the large piece of property. It is said that they chose the location because its breath-taking view reminded them of their homeland.

Maria's story, of course, came to prominence through the movie *The Sound of Music*, which won five Academy Awards, including Best Motion Picture. Soon after the release of the film, Maria and the von Trapp family became international sensations.

In the quaint town of Stowe, the locals knew that the real Maria was a great deal different from Julie Andrews, who portrayed her in the film. Though Maria and Julie were the same height (5'8"), Maria was big-boned and sturdy-looking. She looked like someone who *could* climb every mountain!

Maria could be temperamental and forceful. The woman who became an orphan at age ten had had a tough life. She could be a true force of nature.

The townspeople also mentioned Maria's driving. They told me that Maria had a silver Mercedes convertible. One person joked, "If you ever see a silver Mercedes on the road, you might want to pull over because Maria really likes to zoom around these mountains!"

During the very same summer that I was doing theatre in Vermont, the community theatre in my hometown of Savannah was producing *The Sound of Music*. It just so happened that my sister, Wendy, was playing the role of Maria. I was living in the town of the person my sister was playing. Pretty cool. I had a brainstorm. What if I could get the real Maria to contact my sister? What if I could get the real Maria to write or call Wendy?

The Trapp Family Lodge was open to the public during the day, so I went to see if I could meet and talk with Maria, who was seventy-five years old at the time. I was able to meet her, along with about fifty other people. She was too busy greeting all the tourists for me to have a conversation with her about my sister. How could I talk with Maria in a quieter more private manner?

The Trapp Family Lodge had a very nice restaurant. I thought if I went to eat supper there, I would have a better chance of talking with Maria in private. The restaurant was expensive, but it would be worth it. Little brother would be scoring major points with big sister.

On a night that we did not have a performance, I went to the Trapp Family Lodge for supper. I did not ask any of my theatre friends to go with me because I knew they didn't have the money to spend on a costly dinner. We were starving actors doing summer stock. This was a once-in-a-lifetime chance to do something special for my sister, so I would take the loss, but I couldn't ask my theatre friends to make the same sacrifice. So, I threw on my best clothes and headed to the von Trapps' by myself.

I arrived at the Lodge at seven o'clock and was escorted to a table that was exquisitely set and decorated. This was a "cloth napkin" kind of place. As I sat down, I said to the hostess. "Is it possible for me to talk with Maria for a moment?"

"I'm sorry," she said, "but Maria has already gone to

bed."

I thought, "Gone to bed? No, no, no! She couldn't have gone to bed! It's only seven o'clock! I've got something important to tell her!"

"Oh, okay," I said, trying to smile and be polite.

I was having an expensive meal by myself all for nothing. I ordered the cheapest thing on the menu and ate it as fast as I could. I'm sure it was the cheapest and fastest meal ever served at the Trapp Family Lodge.

I left the restaurant and went outside, feeling sorry for myself. As I walked to the parking lot, I noticed a car that was parked beside the lodge. It was a silver Mercedes convertible, a really nice-looking car.

"That must be the car I heard about," I thought. "This must be Maria's." The car's top was down, everything exposed. People must have been very trusting in the mountains of Vermont.

Then I had an idea. What if I left a note for Maria? What if I explained about Wendy and then put the note in the seat of her prized car? Would Maria find it? Would she read it? Would she do something?

It was worth a try. I found a scrap piece of paper and wrote:

Dear Maria,
    My sister is portraying you in a production of The Sound of Music in Savannah, Georgia. It would thrill her to hear from you. Would you mind writing her at this address?

After I wrote down the address, I placed the note on the

driver's seat.

About a week later, I got a phone call from Savannah. It was my sister. She said, "You won't believe who I just got a letter from today—Maria von Trapp!"

It worked. Maria had found the scrap piece of paper, read the note, and took the time to write Wendy. The trip to the Trapp Family Lodge was not in vain after all.

Thirty-eight years after my visit to the Lodge, I had a von Trapp visit me. Elisabeth von Trapp, Maria's granddaughter, is a wonderful singer and musician. We were fortunate to have Elisabeth come to my church to perform a concert in February of 2018. If you ever get a chance to hear Elisabeth in concert, go. She's marvelous!

As I introduced Elisabeth to the audience, I shared the story about Maria, Wendy, the note, and the silver Mercedes convertible. My sister now lives in New Jersey. She happened to be visiting Savannah when Elisabeth gave her concert, so Wendy got to meet and hear Elisabeth too.

Before the concert, our church supplied a meal for Elisabeth and her husband, Ed, in our Social Hall. So, thirty-eight years after sitting alone eating supper at the Trapp Family Lodge, I got to sit at a table and eat with Maria's granddaughter.

Then we all went into the sanctuary to be blessed by Elisabeth's concert. One of the many highlights was when Elisabeth asked us all to join her in singing "Edelweiss."

I'm sure that over the years there have been people who were disappointed that the real Maria did not look like Julie

Andrews or act exactly how Julie portrayed her on the screen. But, in many ways, Maria was ahead of her time, giving women permission to be strong and assertive. Without her strength and forcefulness, the von Trapp family never would have had the success they had as a singing group. They never would have had the funds and organization to move to the United States. They never would have been able to build a successful business, a place that thousands of people have enjoyed over the years. I am impressed that Maria had this kind of drive, passion, and work ethic but still had the sensitivity and kindheartedness to do things like write to my sister, whom she had never met.

In 1987, Maria died of heart failure at the age of eighty-two. The woman had touched many lives through the film about her, through the music she and her family performed, and through her hospitality at her family home and lodge.

Maria also touched a brother and a sister from Savannah, Georgia—thanks to her silver Mercedes convertible with the top down.

STUDY QUESTIONS

- Have you ever been to the von Trapp Family Lodge in Stowe, Vermont? If so, what was it like for you?

- How did you first learn of Maria von Trapp? Through the film, *The Sound of Music*? Through the play, *The Sound of Music*? Through someone's telling you about her? Through this story?

- How does it impact us when we learn about the human qualities of people we have admired or have put on a pedestal?

- Why are women often judged for being assertive and forceful in ways men would not be judged?

- Twice, Billy tried to talk with Maria about his sister but was unsuccessful. He finally accomplished his goal by placing a note in Maria's car. Have there been times when you were not able to accomplish a goal but later were able to achieve it by thinking out-of-the-box?

- What will you remember most from this story?

LEARNING TO TOUCH

I n 2017, my friend Linda Combs and I drove 458 miles to Tamarac, Florida, for a special friend's birthday. The birthday gal was a former church member, May Johnson. I suppose that ministers are not supposed to have favorite church members, but I must admit that May Johnson is one of mine. May was born on May 25, 1917. I wasn't about to miss her 100th birthday!

❦

Before I met May, I knew her daughter, Kate Jacobson, who was a member of Asbury Memorial. Kate was a respiratory therapist at a nearby hospital, but at Asbury Memorial she was known as "the singer." The petite Kate could pack a punch with her voice and sang all styles of music. She easily could have sung professionally but decided to settle down and raise three children instead.

Kate told us that her mother would be moving to Savannah to be closer to her and the grandkids. We were looking forward to meeting her mom and having her as part of our church family.

In July of 1997, May Johnson arrived in town. The Queens

native had a thick New York accent and a very endearing spirit. But May's transition to Savannah was not an easy one. She felt like a fish out of water. She didn't know many people in Savannah.

One day, May decided to reach out and connect with some of the older members of our church by attending a group that met on Mondays called the "Busy Bees." The Busy Bees formed in the early 1970s and consisted mostly of women who wanted to get together for fellowship. Their excuse for getting together was to make clown dolls that they could sell to help pay the church's bills. The fellowshipping was a success, and the clown making was a success. The Busy Bees have been meeting once a week ever since.

May lived in an apartment complex twelve miles from the church. One Monday, the eighty-year-old got in her car, carefully drove to the church, and parked in the lot to attend her first meeting with the Busy Bees. She got out of the car and started feeling nervous and anxious. She slowly walked to the church door that led from the parking lot into the room where the Busy Bees met. When May opened the door, the members of the group turned their heads in the direction of the door. When May saw everyone looking at her, she panicked. She shut the door, hurried back to her car, and drove all the way back to her apartment.

But May did not give up. She kept coming to church on Sundays. She gradually got to know people, and she eventually joined the Busy Bees. She developed a great group of friends.

May and I also developed a close friendship. We had a couple of things in common: we both had lived in Queens, and we both loved movies. So, we became movie buddies.

On one of our "dates," May shared with me that it took her a while to trust the love and hospitality that she experienced at the church. She also shared that she had never been in an environment where physical affection was shared between friends. She was not used to being touched or hugged. She said, "We never did any of that where I came from."

But after being at Asbury Memorial for a while, she started becoming more comfortable with touch and hugs. She was surprised at this new development. May felt confident enough to become a volunteer at one of our local hospitals where she became very adept at meeting and helping people.

We received sad news that Kate, her husband, Jake, and their children would be moving to south Florida for a job opportunity. Everyone expected May to pack up and join them, but she didn't want to leave Asbury Memorial and all of her hugging friends. She stayed in Savannah two more years before deciding it was time to live closer to family. In 2002, off to Florida she went. About three months later, I received this incredible letter from May:

Hey Billy,

Just a note to let you know that I am thinking of you and all of the folks at Asbury. Also, I just had to let you know how the things I learned from you and the people at church have affected my life here in Florida.

As you know, I am volunteering in the emergency room at University Hospital. My responsibility is to reassure the patients when they come in that they will be getting the best care possible. *I try to make them comfortable—bring a warm blanket if they are cold, bring coffee, a soda, or whatever to the patient's family. But the important thing I have learned from you and the folks at Asbury is the importance of contact. I check on them as often as I can, reassure them with a touch on the shoulder—or so many of them reach out so that you can hold their hands. It calms them down when they are apprehensive.*

As I've told you, I was never a hugger or a toucher until I came to Asbury. And now, because I realized how comforting this approach to people can be, I can help people.

Last week, I was walking past the bed of a new patient, a tiny African-American lady about eighty-five years of age. She motioned to me and I went to her bed.

I could barely understand her. She was so weak. But finally, I realized that she wanted water. I checked with a doctor, and then brought her some water and held the cup while she drank through the straw.

She was in the Emergency Room for a long, long time, and when I had a chance I would stop and help her to drink. After they decided to admit her, I went back to her while she was waiting for her room to be prepared upstairs. She was a little agitated and in pain and I held her hand. But suddenly, without thinking about what I was doing, I found myself running my fingers through her hair as I always did with my children when they were upset.

As she drifted off to sleep I could hear her say softly, "Thank you...oh, thank you...thank you."

As they wheeled her away, I suddenly realized how I have grown. Of course, I do other things—file reports, answer the phone, run errands—but I enjoy the contact with patients and their families the most.

Give my love to everyone at Asbury!

May

When Linda Combs and I went to see May to celebrate her 100th birthday, we learned that films had played an important part of my movie buddy's life. After being born in New York City in 1917, little five-year-old May Kaiser starred in the silent film *Silver Wings*, directed by Edward Carewe and John Ford. Search for it, and you can see a wonderful picture of little May sitting in the lap of Mary Carr, an actress who was in 144 movies. By the way, May's film mother, Mary Carr, had good genes, too. She lived to be ninety-nine.

As we celebrated May's birthday, we asked her if she had any advice about how to live a long life. She said, "Walk every day. I walked a mile every day until I was ninety-seven years old."

I think May also could have added that part of her success in living was her openness to growth and to learning new things. For when she was an octogenarian, she learned how to touch people in healthy and meaningful ways.

God bless you, May Kaiser Johnson. We love you. Thank you for touching our lives.

STUDY QUESTIONS

- Did you grow up in an environment where physical affection was expressed between friends? What was that like?

- How do you know when healthy touching or hugging is okay and not invading someone's personal space?

- Describe a circumstance where healthy touch has helped you?

- Describe a circumstance where you have helped someone through touch?

- Are you open to new areas of growth in your life? If so, what are you doing to stretch and grow?

- What other lessons can we learn from this story about the great May Johnson and her life?

- May attributed her success to walking a mile every day. What do you do regularly to be happy and successful?

- What will you remember most from this story?

LET IT GO!

I n the 1950s, '60s, and '70s, my grandmother, Sue Hester, lived on the May River in Bluffton, South Carolina. Bluffton was a quaint fishing village, a stone's throw from Hilton Head Island and only twenty-three miles from my hometown of Savannah. My cousins and I loved to go to Bluffton during the summer, so we could see our "Gramma" and go swimming, fishing, and crabbing. It was a wonderful way to live, especially for youngsters. We were a bunch of Huck Finns!

My cousins' parents, my Uncle Bob and Aunt Marge, had a summer house next door to my grandmother's house. So, my cousins spent more time at Bluffton than I did and became excellent boaters. Whenever I went over to Bluffton and we needed the boat, they would take charge.

One summer day when I was thirteen, I went over to Bluffton; to my surprise, none of my cousins were there. I really wanted to go crabbing, but no one was there to handle my Uncle Bob's boat. Uncle Bob was a dentist in Savannah. It was a weekday, so he, of course, was at work.

The boat was already on the water, tied to my

grandmother's dock. Looking at it, sitting nicely on the river on a beautiful day, I thought, "Billy, you are now a teenager. You should be able to handle the boat." After all, I had watched my uncle and cousins drive the boat a "million" times. I wouldn't do anything fancy—just take the boat out for a nice, slow ride. If I felt comfortable in it, I then would use it to go crabbing.

There was just one problem: the motor was not on the boat; it was in the boathouse. It would need to be taken out and rolled down the dock on a dolly and then attached to the boat. But again, I had seen my uncle and cousins attach the motor many times before. I could do it.

Using a dolly, I rolled the big, heavy Evinrude motor out of the boathouse and down to the dock where the boat was tied. I unfastened the motor and got a good grip on it. Then, with one leg on the dock and the other leg in the boat, I picked up the motor to swing it from the dock over to the boat.

What I did not take into consideration was how much slack there was in the rope that tied off the boat to the dock. What happened next looked like Wile E. Coyote on *The Road Runner Show*. As I tried to swing the motor over from the dock to the boat, the boat started moving away from the dock. While holding the heavy motor, my legs started doing a split—a spread-eagle. As the boat kept moving farther and farther away from the dock, there was just one way to go: down! The motor and I fell into the water.

I was in shock. I had just dropped my uncle's expensive motor into the river. I held onto the dock with my left hand and held the motor with the other. How could I get the motor into the boat before it sank to the bottom of the river?

To my surprise, the motor seemed to be floating, but reality quickly set in as the motor started taking on water and began to sink. The motor pulled me down as it got heavier and heavier. It was hard for me to keep my head above water as I continued to try to hold on to the dock and to the motor. But now, I could no longer keep my face out of the water to get air.

It was then that I started thinking, "Okay, I have a choice. What would be worse—to keep holding onto the motor and go down with it or to let it go and have to tell my uncle that his motor is at the bottom of the river?" That was a no brainer. I was going down with the motor!

As I was struggling to hold on to the motor and trying to get my face above water to gasp some air, I heard a voice: "Billy! Let go! Let go! Let go of the motor!" Looking at the surface from under the water, I could see a blue sky and a figure on the dock. It was my Aunt Marge. She was on her knees with her head bent down to the water as she shouted, "Billy! Let it go! Let go of the motor! Let it go!"

Since I am alive and sharing this story, I obviously followed my aunt's advice and let go. The motor sank to the bottom of the river. Exhausted, I slowly climbed onto the dock, knowing that I had really messed up.

Fortunately, my uncle's brother, my Uncle Bruddie, lived nearby. He was a massive man and an expert seaman. He came over to the dock and somehow hooked the motor with a grappling hook and lifted it out of the water by himself. This was an incredible feat since the motor was at the bottom of the river in murky salt water and the water's weight made the motor even heavier.

Let It Go!

After Uncle Bruddie rescued the motor from the river, we took it to the boat shop to dry out. But even after this emergency treatment, the motor never would be the same. Motors are not meant to live on the bottom of salt water rivers.

The first time I saw my Uncle Bob after the incident, he didn't say anything to me about it. He didn't have to. I knew how much he loved his boats and motors. For a long time, every time I was around him, I kept waiting for him to tell me that I should have known better—to tell me never to do it again. But he never mentioned it.

That really didn't surprise me. Uncle Bob was a top-notch fella *and* a top-notch Methodist who knew all about grace.

I never did ask my aunt how she knew that I was in trouble. The dock I was on was not directly in front of her house. But somehow, she was at the right place at the right time. I am thankful for her reminding me to "let it go." It's hard to explain what her words meant to me as I was struggling in the water. They reminded me that I was more important—more valuable—than the expensive motor.

My Aunt Marge has passed away, but I need to continue hearing her words. I need to let go of regrets—let go of shame—let go of things that pull me down.

Perhaps we all could benefit from picturing a metaphorical image of God kneeling down and begging us to let go of the things that pull us down and prevent us from experiencing life.

STUDY QUESTIONS

- Why is it so difficult to let go of something?

- Is there something you need to let go of?

- What will happen to you if you don't let go of it?

- What will happen if you do let go?

- Have you ever played the role of Aunt Marge for someone? In what way?

- Who are the Aunt Marges in your life—people who remind you to let go?

- How does it feel to imagine God encouraging you to let go?

- What will you remember most from this story?

Mrs. Upchurch and the Young Couple

When I came to Asbury Memorial in 1993, the church was about to close. The once-thriving church with a large congregation only had around twenty-five active members. The youngest member was sixty-six years old, and the average age was eighty.

These twenty-five people did not huddle up and sit together in Asbury Memorial's large sanctuary; they did not clump together. We are creatures of habit so these twenty-five sat in the same pew they had been sitting in for many years. At one time, they had been sitting with spouses and children and grandchildren surrounding them. But now, their family members had died, moved away, or simply stopped attending church. So, these twenty-five souls were scattered throughout this large sanctuary—one here, another there, two or three sitting together over there. From the pulpit area where I stood, it looked like a huge empty space with some dots here and there.

One of the dots was a woman named Lerah Upchurch, a true "steel magnolia." In her eighties, Lerah always was kind and supportive. She was a widow and had been a member of Asbury Memorial for most of her life. She always sat by herself, to my left about ten rows back—the spot where she and her husband sat for all those many years, Sunday after Sunday.

A handful of new people started attending our worship services so we got a sprinkling of more dots in the pews. Two of those dots were a young couple named Jerry and Anne-Liesse Ankeny. When they first started attending Asbury Memorial, they happened to sit close to where Lerah was sitting. Week after week, I got used to seeing those three dots in the same general area.

Near the end of 1996, Lerah became ill; and she suddenly passed away in January of 1997. I wasn't sure if Jerry and Anne-Liesse knew Lerah, but since they always sat close to each other, I called them to let them know of Lerah's death.

"Did we know Lerah?" they exclaimed. "We thought you knew that she became one of our closest friends."

They went on to tell me that on their first visit to the church, Lerah introduced herself and invited them to her house for supper. They started to be in touch with each other on a regular basis. Whenever Jerry and Anne-Liesse missed church or if Lerah ever missed church, which was rare, they would call to check on each other.

The Ankenys told me that Lerah almost always got to church before they did. But on one particular Sunday, the Ankenys beat Lerah to church. They sat in their usual place and waited for Lerah to come sit beside them. However, they did not realize that they were actually off by one row of pews. Lerah came into the sanctuary, sat down beside them, and whispered, "Well, my husband probably wouldn't mind me sitting in a different place just one time."

About eighteen years ago, Anne-Liesse became pregnant and gave birth to a daughter named Sarrah Elisabeth. That evening I went to the hospital room to meet little Sarrah. I sat down with the new mom and dad and experienced all the joy and wonder that surrounded us in the room. It was a magical moment.

Jerry, who was one of the proudest new fathers I had ever seen, said to me, "You know, Billy, I think Lerah Upchurch saved our marriage."

I remembered that six or so years earlier, Jerry had come to the office to see me. He shared that he and Anne-Liesse were struggling and needed some help. I tried giving him a pep talk and gave him a referral to a marriage counselor, but I didn't know what the outcome had been. I only knew that Jerry and Anne-Liesse were still hanging in there together, and now, a number of years later—a child.

I was curious about Jerry's comment about Lerah and the effect she had on their marriage. After he said, "I think Lerah Upchurch saved our marriage," I said to Jerry, "How so? What do you mean?"

From her hospital bed, Anne-Liesse piped in, "Jerry's right. Lerah meant so much to us and did a lot for us. I think she could tell that we were struggling. She had us over to her house for dinner a couple of times. She'd share some of her wisdom with us, but mostly we learned by just being with her. We learned a lot by the way she talked about her husband. She loved him so much. It made us think. It made us realize that we had taken each other for granted and that we needed to appreciate each other more."

Before leaving the hospital that night, I took one final look at little Sarrah. I left in awe and in wonder as I realized that a little lady at Asbury Memorial had something to do with the creation of this child—through her kindness, through her giving, through her sharing, through her connecting. I was in awe that out of this trinitarian relationship of Jerry, Anne-Liesse, and Lerah grew another trinitarian relationship of Jerry, Anne-Liesse, and little Sarrah.

Not long after the birth, the Ankenys moved to North Carolina due to a job opportunity. I've only seen them two or three times in eighteen years. But a couple of months ago, I got a letter from their house in North Carolina; however, it was not from Jerry or Anne-Liesse. It was from Sarrah, who was graduating from high school—an invitation to little Sarrah's graduation.

I wanted to share this story in a sermon, so I emailed Anne-Liesse to see if that would be okay with them. She wrote back:

> *"I am so honored to be associated with Mrs. Upchurch. I learned so much from her, perhaps much more than she intended me/us to learn, especially about commitment and faithfulness. She changed my life."*

Anne-Liesse also wrote that dance had become a big part of Sarrah's life. Sarrah started dancing in the second grade and just recently had performed in her very last dance recital before going to the University of North Carolina in Chapel

Hill. There, she would major in Biology, with the hope of one day being a pediatrician.

❧

The influence of one woman continues. A little eighty-five-year-old woman sitting in a church pew changed lives, changed the future, and affected the lives of people for generations.

Do we realize the power we have?

Do we realize the power we have with those around us?

Do we realize the power we have to shape lives — to shape the future?

STUDY QUESTIONS

- Why do so many of us get attached to sitting in the same place in church or in school?

- Are you attached to a certain seat somewhere? Where and why?

- Why do you think Lerah and the Ankenys developed such a close relationship?

- How do you think the Ankenys benefitted from this relationship? How did it help their marriage?

- Do you have friendships with people from other generations? What advantages are there in having such relationships?

- Have you ever considered how a single act of kindness can affect lives—even future generations? Can you think of any examples of that happening in your life?

- What will you remember most from this story?

"THE PABLO"

C heri and I rarely have anyone over to our house. In fact, Cheri and I don't have a house. Our dogs have a house, and they let us live there.

It didn't start that way. When we first moved to Savannah in 1991, we got a little rescue dog named "Toto," who looked more like Toto than Toto did. In fact, our Toto starred in two separate stage productions of *The Wizard of Oz*. One was at the Savannah Civic Center. He got excellent reviews in the newspaper.

After Toto lived to be about 103, he died; and we got a new rescue dog—a mix that was mostly Yellow Lab. We named him "Simon," but we should have named him "Jesus," because he was the most loving, good-natured dog the world has ever seen.

Wendell, one of our twin sons, had always wanted a Chihuahua, so as Christmas approached, Cheri and I found a rescue Chihuahua listed in the paper. We wanted to check it out before we surprised Wendell on Christmas morning, so we arranged to go meet the dog and see what it was like.

It was being kept temporarily at a person's house, so we had to figure out how to go see the dog without our little boys knowing about it. They were about eight years old at the time.

Their best friend was and continues to be a boy named Colin Harrison. The three of them grew up together and are still like the "Three Amigos," even in their twenties. We called Colin's parents, Geoff and Susan Harrison, to see if they could pick up our boys and take them over to their house so Cheri and I could secretly check out the dog.

The Harrisons picked up the boys, and Cheri and I hurried to our car. "What street are we going to?" I asked.

She took out a little piece of paper and said, "Let's see. It's on East 48th Street."

I said, "48th Street? Don't the Harrisons live on 48th Street?"

"How about that?" she said. "But 48th is a long street. It's probably not near their house."

We kept driving to the address, and we got closer and closer to the Harrisons' house. The house with the dog ended up being three houses from the Harrisons'. We sent the boys to go off somewhere in the city of Savannah so we could check out the dog, and the dog ended up being seventy yards away from where we sent them. What were the chances of that?

When we pulled up to the house, we actually saw the boys, who were playing in the Harrisons' front yard. Cheri and I had to park behind a car, so they wouldn't see us. We were hiding behind bushes as we sneaked to the house with the dog. We got inside and met the Chihuahua. He seemed fine, so we arranged to pick him up at a later date.

"The Pablo"

Then on Christmas morning, we gave the Chihuahua to Wendell, and he promptly named it "Pablo Sanchez Taco Bell Hester."

❦

Many Chihuahuas have an inferiority complex due to their small stature, so they overcompensate by being overly aggressive and domineering. "Pablo" got an extra dose of this inferiority complex. He always had to have his ego stroked, always had to be the Alpha dog, always had to out-mark the bigger dog, Simon. And Simon, being the good Christian dog that he was, would not retaliate. Pablo was like a flea to Simon. Simon could have blown little Pablo away with a sneeze, but Simon would just smile and say, "Let the little guy have his way. He needs it." The giant dog and the tiny dog were quite the pair.

But life would get more challenging for Pablo. A few years later, our other twin, Wesley, wanted a dog. Along came a rescue Beagle named "Angel." Pablo now had to rule over and out-mark two dogs.

❦

Years passed, and Cheri and I took the boys to college in Valdosta, Georgia. As we were traveling through Waycross, Georgia, on the way home, a dog was in the middle of the road, standing right in front of us. It had no collar, but a ton of fleas. There were no houses in the area, so we could not find its owner. We decided to take it home, clean it up, and send a message back to Waycross saying that we'd cleaned up someone's dog and were ready to give it back. There were no takers.

In the meantime, my wife's parents got very sick and

needed to move into a nursing home, so we had to take their dog.

If you are counting, that was five. Five dogs.

That meant Pablo had four dogs to rule over—four dogs to out-mark, which, he would want me to tell you, was not a problem for him. When the dogs went outside to do their business, Pablo stared them down. After the dogs finished, he went over and marked on every single spot. He even doubled-back and did it again—just so everyone got the message. How that little body held so much fluid, I'll never know.

Of course, this kind of attitude often got Pablo in trouble, especially when you consider that one of our newer dogs was never house-trained and often did his business inside the house. Now, if one of the dogs did its business inside, guess who was not going to be outdone? Pablo had to do it too! (Now you know why people rarely came over to our house!)

Pablo knew better! But he didn't care! Because it was all about Pablo, all about his ego!

Whenever I caught him doing something like marking inside the house or taking another dog's treat, I got mad and raised my voice, saying, "Pablo!"

When I said, "Pablo!" in my serious tone, Pablo knew he'd done something really wrong. He knew he was in big trouble! And what did Pablo do?

Did he run? Did he growl or snap at me?

Nope, not Pablo.

Every time the great, mighty Pablo got into trouble— every time I was really mad at him—he stopped in his tracks, flipped over on his back, and put his little legs in the air with the wrists of his front paws down in the most defenseless, vulnerable position possible.

All I could see was his ugly, pink stomach and his tiny head above it. It was as if he was saying, "Take me! Take me! Take me! My life is in your hands."

What do you do with that?

I could do absolutely nothing. I just stood there, and my anger dissipated as I looked at the cutest, most vulnerable thing alive.

Pablo was one smart dog. He knew how to disarm me and my anger. And before you knew it, I found myself picking up the little dog and hugging him.

Pablo knew that showing vulnerability at the right place and at the right time may well have been the strongest thing he could ever do.

The apostle Paul was a lot like Pablo. One ancient Greek text describes Paul as, "A man of middling size, and his hair was scanty, and his legs were a little crooked, and his knees were far apart; he had large eyes, and his eyebrows met, and his nose was somewhat long" — sounds a lot like Pablo to me!

And, like Pablo, Paul had a bit of an ego. He needed to have one if he hoped to spread the Christian message all over the known world. But Paul was also smart like Pablo. He knew that he was at his best when he was vulnerable. He knew how important it was to do "The Pablo." "Therefore," he said, "I am content with weaknesses, insults, hardships, persecutions, and calamities for the sake of Christ; for whenever I am weak, then I am strong" (2 Corinthians 12:10).

WOW! Wisdom

Two years ago, our wonderful, faithful Lab, Simon, left us and made his transition. It was hard on Pablo without Simon to boss around. With his own age and ailments, we almost lost Pablo several times, but he was just too stubborn and too egotistical to die. He wasn't going to leave his domain to the other three dogs.

But after seeing Pablo in so much pain, we eventually had to put Pablo to sleep. He is now with the gentle giant—his good friend, Simon.

❦

But Pablo was right.

And Simon was right.

And the apostle Paul was right.

When we are weak, when we are vulnerable, then we are strong.

Let us always try to remember to do "The Pablo."

STUDY QUESTIONS

- If you could be a dog, what kind of dog would you want to be and why?

- When Pablo did something wrong and got in trouble, why did it lessen Billy's anger when Pablo did "The Pablo"?

- How is there power in vulnerability?

- The apostle Paul's statement "When I am weak, then I am strong" is a paradox. Can you think of ways this paradox has occurred in your life?

- What keeps us from doing "The Pablo" (in other words, being vulnerable)?

- Try to think of one thing you can do to be better at doing "The Pablo"? Who might help you along the way?

- What will you remember most from this story?

GOING THE DISTANCE

I n 1996, I had the opportunity to attend the Summer Olympics in Atlanta with my father-in-law, Thurman Butcher, and my brother-in-law, Pat Ciccodicola. We had the pleasure of seeing sprinter Michael Johnson win a gold medal and set a new world record in one of the most electrifying events I've ever attended. We also got to see decathlete Dan O'Brien come out on top after those ten grueling contests in the Decathlon, as he too won a Gold Medal. But the athlete who stood out to many of us that day was a little-known Italian runner named Stefano Baldini.

In the 10,000-meter race (which is a little over six miles), Baldini finished dead last. A man from Ethiopia won the race in record time. But Stefano Baldini was impressive because seven of the twenty-five runners did not even finish. They pulled out during the race because of a cramp or for some other reason. Next to their names were the letters "DNF" (Did Not Finish). Some just went over to the side of the track and slumped over. But not Baldini.

After the first few miles, it was clear that Baldini was in last place. He was running so slowly that the runners started to lap him. The lead runners lapped him once, and then twice, until every runner lapped him at least two times.

While Baldini was running the last mile of the race, the scores of the other runners were already being tabulated. Their times were already being analyzed, and the medals were already being brought in. But as Stefano Baldini went around the track, the announcer told the people in the stadium that Baldini was running the last mile faster than he ran any other mile of the race. The announcer also said, "Baldini's time has been going down every mile." In other words, he was running the last mile faster than the first! When he crossed the finish line, the crowd in that big stadium burst into loud applause.

I once read a sermon by a minister who had seen the same race. It was so long ago, I can't remember who the minister was, but I remember that he said how impressed he was with Baldini's staying power.

The minister asked, "How do we keep pressing on when we find ourselves in last place?" How do you keep going when you know that you're not going to medal? How do you find the strength to keep on keeping on when the journey is difficult? The minister said, "Why aren't more books written about completing the journey, and not just finishing, but giving your very best all the way to the end?"

Eight years later, on August 30, 2004, I prepared to take a morning bath. I usually take a shower, but it was a Monday morning, and the day before had been an especially taxing day at the church. Monday was my day off, so I really wanted to relax. I got the *Savannah Morning News* to read while I was soaking. As I was flipping through the pages of the newspaper, I saw an article about the closing ceremony of the 2004 Summer Olympics, which had just ended—the closing ceremony was on Sunday, the night before.

There was a picture of a man who had won the last medal for the United States at the Olympics, which was why he had his picture in the paper. He won the medal in the grueling 26-mile Marathon. I could not remember the runner's name, but I looked it up. Are you ready for this? His name was Mebrahtom Keflezighi. He's called "Meb" for short. In my research, I later learned that Meb won the New York City Marathon in 2009, and he won the Boston Marathon in 2014, becoming the first American man to win both races since 1983.

But on this Monday morning in 2004, I'm reading about him because he won the Silver Medal in the marathon—he came in second. As I soaked in the tub and continued to read the article, I couldn't believe the words I read next: "The Gold Medal was won by Italian runner Stefano Baldini."

Stefano Baldini? Stefano Baldini? The man who came in last in 1996? The man who kept being lapped by the other runners? He came in first?

I couldn't believe it! The man who came in last place eight years earlier came in first place and won the Gold Medal!

❦

Now you know why I remember taking this particular bath! I could never forget the man—the Gold Medal winner—who came in last but finished well.

May we all finish well.

STUDY QUESTIONS

- Have you ever been to the Olympics? If so, what was the experience like?

- What's the most thrilling sports event you've attended? What made it so exciting?

- What metaphorical races are you currently running? What's your most important race?

- How are you at "finishing well"?

- How would you describe diligence? Or discipline? Or perseverance? How would you rate yourself in these areas? What could you do to be better in these areas?

- Is there anything else we can learn from the incredible determination and career of Stefano Baldini?

- What will you remember most from this story?

SANCTUARY

When I was sixteen years old, a friend encouraged me to check out a new church that had started in Savannah. I already was a member of a church and was very involved with that faith community. The new church, however, offered a service during the week, so I was able to attend my regular church on Sunday and still experience the other church at a midweek service.

I drove to the address of the church for a worship service. It wasn't a typical church building. It seemed more like a large house. There were about fifty-five people in attendance. I didn't know much about the church, but as the service started and as the preacher preached, it soon became obvious that it was a Pentecostal church. Throughout much of the service, people were praising God and speaking in tongues.

❦

If you're not familiar with speaking in tongues, don't worry. There is a lot of confusion, and there are differences of opinion on the subject. For some people, speaking in tongues means that someone has been given a special message from God. The person shares this message in a language that

74

cannot be understood by most people. However, when the message is shared in a public setting, another person should be present who is able to understand the language and communicate what is being said.

Other people believe that speaking in tongues has to do with a person's personal prayer life. When someone communes with God, that person expresses himself or herself through an unknown language that makes them feel closer to God. An interpreter is not involved.

This congregation seemed to be blending these two understandings. People were speaking in tongues, but there was no interpreter. People seemed to be using the language for their own connection with God but were doing so in public.

Some Christians believe that speaking in tongues was something people experienced in the days of the early church but that it no longer exists.

Then, finally, there are many other Christians who don't believe in speaking in tongues at all.

Needless to say, there is a wide range of interpretations about what speaking in tongues actually is, and there is a variety of beliefs in regard to its existence. So, however you feel about speaking in tongues, you'll find others who agree with you.

❦

The new church I was attending was led by a female pastor, which was very rare in the South in the 1970s. At the end of the worship service, the minister said, "Everyone should be able to speak in tongues. It's a gift God wants you to have. And if you don't have it, come forward and I will help you receive the gift." I was just sixteen years old, and I didn't know about all the different understandings and interpretations about speaking in tongues. I just heard the minister say, "This is something that will help you feel closer to God."

Well I figured that, if this was something God wanted people to have, if it was something that could draw a person closer to God, then why not have it?

I decided to go forward. One other person, a woman, came forward also. Everyone else already appeared to be able to speak in tongues.

The minister put her hands on the woman's head and offered a prayer. Then the pastor turned the woman around to face the congregation and said, "Speak!" The woman opened her mouth, and she started speaking in tongues. Everyone responded by praising God!

Now it was my turn. Everyone got really quiet again.

The minister put her hands on my head and offered a very impressive prayer. Then she turned me around to face the congregation and said, "Speak!"

Unknown to the minister was the fact that nothing in my mind (or in my tongue) had changed. Everything seemed to be the same. I felt the same. But I saw every person in the room staring at me with eager anticipation. They just knew I was going to speak in tongues.

I didn't know what to do. If I didn't speak in tongues, there was going to be a lot of disappointed people. I would be a disappointment. They might even think something was wrong with me. What if they thought I didn't have enough faith?

I wish I had had the strength and the nerve to be honest with everyone. I wish I had said something like, "I'm sorry, folks. I guess it didn't happen this time."

But I didn't have the strength or nerve. Tapping into my acting skills, I decided that I would fake it. I would pretend to speak in tongues. So, I opened my mouth and tried making some sounds that I heard on an episode of *Tarzan*.

Right when I opened my mouth and made my very first sound, everyone started praising God—loudly! Which was a good thing, because if they had really listened to me, they would have heard the worst impression of speaking in tongues they had ever heard!

I then walked out of the church as fast as I could, got in my car, and breathed a sigh of relief that I was no longer in that place. It was a horrible, horrible experience. And it happened at a church.

Peer pressure can be harmful and destructive because it encourages us not to be ourselves—not to be authentic. The worst place in the world for one to experience peer pressure is the church. The church, of all places, is where we should be able to be ourselves—to be authentic.

Unfortunately, the universal church historically hasn't done a very good job at letting people have breathing room. It has left little room for questions, little room for doubt, little room for the movement of God's spirit in a person's life. Throughout history, people have been ridiculed, judged, persecuted, and even killed for questioning and doubting. I think it's one reason why so many people no longer attend church. They have been hurt by feeling forced to believe something, think something, or do something. One of the great sins of the church happens when we do not give people the freedom to be themselves, doubts and all.

That's why one of my favorite Sundays of the year is the Sunday after Easter when we remember the story of Thomas, who was not mocked or judged for not believing that the disciples had seen Jesus after his death. In fact, it was Thomas' questioning that seemed to have drawn Jesus back to the group, so Thomas could have a first-hand experience of the resurrected Jesus.

The Sunday after Easter is sometimes called "Quasimodo Sunday." You may recall that the main character in Victor Hugo's book *The Hunchback of Notre Dame* was named Quasimodo. The day was not named after the character in the novel; rather, the character was named after the day. On the Sunday after Easter, the early church used to celebrate those who were newly baptized. They would sing a Gregorian chant: "*Quasi modo genti infants, alleluia!*" (as newborn babies, alleluia!).

Victor Hugo wrote about a very deformed newborn baby being left and abandoned on the steps of the Cathedral of Notre Dame. The child was found the Sunday after Easter, on Quasimodo Sunday, so he was given the name "Quasimodo." The child was brought into the cathedral and raised where he had sanctuary. No one could harm him.

But whenever he left the cathedral, Quasimodo was ridiculed and beaten due to his appearance. Fortunately, he could return to the cathedral for safety and protection.

❦

The church should always be a safe place for people—a

Sanctuary

place where everyone can be open and honest—a place to be themselves—a place to have sanctuary.

STUDY QUESTIONS

- Is there a place where you feel that you have sanctuary? If so, where?

- What would you have done if you had been in Billy's shoes after the minister prayed for him to speak in tongues?

- Why did Billy pretend to speak in tongues?

- Have you ever felt forced to believe something or do something in the name of God or religion? What happened?

- In what ways have you felt that you have sanctuary at your place of worship?

- How can you help make your place of worship a safe place for people?

- What will you remember most from this story?

THE SUBWAY SUPERHERO

A round 1984, I went to Toronto, Canada, to visit my future wife, Cheri. We were seriously courting each other at the time. We both were living in New York, but she was touring in the musical *Joseph and the Amazing Technicolor Dreamcoat*, and the show was currently in Canada.

After experiencing a wonderful trip to Toronto, I flew back to New York. A bus at the airport took me and other passengers into Manhattan and dropped us off at Grand Central Station. I lived in Queens and would have taken a cab from Grand Central to my Queens apartment, but it was 5:30—rush hour. I would have gotten stuck in traffic, and the cab ride would have cost me a fortune.

I went into Grand Central Station to take the subway to Queens. The closest subways were on the lower levels of Grand Central so down the stairs I went, carrying a huge suitcase with one hand and a smaller bag with the other. When I got to the bottom of the stairway, I realized that a train was already at the platform with its doors wide open. The doors would be closing any second. I instinctively jumped from the stairs to the platform, so I could hop on the subway. I had forgotten how packed the subway would be at rush hour. Everyone was squashed in like sardines. As I hopped inside the crowded car, the door closed. There was just one problem: my left arm did not make it inside. My arm was stuck in the door with a huge suitcase dangling from it.

I did not panic. I had ridden enough subways to know that when someone or something got stuck in the door, the conductors somehow knew to reopen the doors. In all my years living in New York, I had never seen a train start moving if the doors weren't completely closed. That was until then.

To my surprise, the train began to move, and the conductor announced the next stop. The train started to leave the platform as it picked up speed. I was in shock and didn't know what to do. Should I drop my suitcase and lose everything in it so I could pull my arm back in? Or should I hang onto the suitcase and risk having my arm torn off?

That sounded like a "no brainer." But at the time, I wasn't sure what to do! I saw that we were fast approaching the end of the station, where the wall of the tunnel suddenly jagged out closer to the subway. Would it take off my arm or hand? It would certainly strip me of my suitcase. I started shouting something about my arm being outside the door. We were just about at the critical point where my arm would be hitting the interior wall of the tunnel. All of a sudden, the wheels of the train started squealing loudly; and the train made a sudden halt. Someone had pulled the emergency brake.

Remember, people are packed in the subway car. They have been working all day. They are tired, cranky, ready to be home—now! When the subway screeched to a halt, everyone started booing. Most of them didn't know why we had stopped. Most people didn't know about my arm. All they knew was that somebody had pulled the emergency brake.

I did not realize it at the time, but every subway car has an emergency brake. Whenever an emergency brake on a subway is pulled, a conductor must check every brake on every car. So, it wasn't just a matter of opening the door and letting me get my arm and suitcase inside. This wasn't going to be, "Okay, he's in now. We can get going again." This was going to take some time. People were not pleased.

I felt horrible about it. It was my fault. I was so appreciative of the person who pulled the brake, but I didn't know who it was. The subway was too crowded for me to see the person. Plus, when the brake was pulled, I was focused on my arm that was about to be ripped off.

I know the person did not want to pull the brake. I know the person wanted to get home. And I know the person did not want people booing them or being mad at them for stopping the train. But that act of courage and compassion may have saved my life—and definitely my arm.

To this day, I don't know who the person was. One of my fantasies about the afterlife is that we will have the opportunity to meet and express gratitude to people who have helped us along the way—especially those we didn't get a chance to thank on earth. I hope I get to meet and thank this good Samaritan one day.

I've often wondered what would have happened if that particular person had not been there that day? What would have happened had this person not been so compassionate, so brave, so loving?

Thank you, good Samaritan, whoever and wherever you are. Thank God for people like you who do the right thing, even when it is difficult to do so. I pray that I can do the same.

STUDY QUESTIONS

- Have you ever been in a situation when your life was suddenly in danger? What happened?

- Have you ever been in a situation where you panicked?

- Have you ever been helped by someone whose identity you don't know?

- Would you have been able to pull the emergency break even though you were surrounded by people who would not have been pleased?

- Why do you think the person who pulled the emergency break never made him or herself known to Billy?

- How can we develop the strength to do the right thing even though it may not be the popular thing to do?

- What will you remember most from this story?

Mr. Mohini

I n 1980—almost forty years ago—I was cast in the role of Jesus in the musical *Godspell*. It was my junior year at Valdosta State College in Valdosta, Georgia. The show was not a period piece like *The Lion in Winter* or *Guys and Dolls*, so the show's director, Dr. Michael Richey, encouraged each cast member to create a costume for our character on our own.

The traditional costume for Jesus in *Godspell* looks like a cross between a clown and Superman. It's basically a clown costume with a Superman shirt. The most difficult part of creating the costume would be finding an appropriate shirt. It needed to be a skin-tight, turquoise-colored pullover with long sleeves. This was before everyone had computers and could find anything and everything online. Making it more challenging was the fact that it was spring, so all the stores were stocked only with short sleeve shirts.

I couldn't find any shirt that would work at the stores in Valdosta. I thought I'd have a better chance in Savannah, so I drove home one weekend for the search. But I didn't have much luck in Savannah either. I couldn't find anything at the mall or at any of the department stores. My last hope was Broughton Street, a downtown street known for its various shops.

As I walked down Broughton Street, I saw a store sign that read: "Mohini's New York Boutique." I had never been in this particular store. I peeked through the store window and saw clothes I rarely saw or wore. They were funky, stylish clothes. I'd give it a try. What did I have to lose?

When I went inside the store, a short, debonair-looking man with thick, dark hair greeted me (think of a shorter Freddie Prinze). He was dressed to the hilt. He had a suave, sophisticated manner about himself as he spoke with an Indian accent. He was very, very personable. When he asked how he could help me, I looked up, and lo and behold, there was the shirt! Tacked to the wall was a long sleeve, skin-tight, turquoise-colored pullover. I tried it on. It fit me like a glove. It was perfect!

During our conversation, I learned that Mr. Mohini just recently had opened his store. He had moved to the United States from India. He had to leave his wife and two children behind until he could get established in America. Then his family would come join him. He said he had not seen his wife and children for many months and that he missed them terribly.

I went back to Valdosta with my new shirt. *Godspell* was incredibly successful. People loved the production. Lines gathered around our fine-arts building with people wanting to see the production two or three times.

I was thankful that Mr. Mohini had the shirt that I couldn't find anywhere else. When I visited Savannah, I made sure to drop by to tell him how successful his shirt had been. After I graduated from college and was moving to New York, I went by Mohini's New York Boutique to have the stylish shop owner pick out some shirts for me to wear at auditions in New York.

Soon after I arrived in the Big Apple, I had a professional photographer take new headshots of me. These would be pictures I would take to auditions along with my résumé. I made sure to wear one of Mr. Mohini's shirts to the photo shoot.

I also had my 8x10 headshot made into postcard-sized pictures, so I could mail them to agents periodically. I took one of the postcard pictures and mailed it to Mohini's New York Boutique. I wanted Mr. Mohini to know that I was now in New York and that I had my headshot taken wearing one of his shirts.

A couple of years passed. On one of my visits to Savannah, I went down to Broughton Street to see Mr. Mohini. By now, he was well established. His wife and children had made it to America and were with him.

Then more years passed as I lived in New York. But I never went back to see Mr. Mohini on my sporadic visits to Savannah.

❦

After I moved back to Savannah in 1991, I wasn't sure if Mohini's New York Boutique was still there, and I really didn't explore it. I was a bit embarrassed. I had planned to go to New York and become a star, not just for me, but for people like Mr. Mohini—people who had helped me along the way. He probably wouldn't understand about my going into the ministry. I might be a bit of a disappointment. I couldn't imagine the reunion being a very positive experience.

As years passed, I still wondered about Mr. Mohini. Had he gone out of business? Sometimes it seemed like I would see the shop; at other times, I didn't. Even if the business was still there, was he still the owner? Had he sold it? Was he still in Savannah? Was he still alive?

Part of me really wanted to see him. But something happened that made me resist pursuing the reunion.

Around 1993, during one of my sermons, I mentioned the name of a friend of mine from my days in junior high school, an African-American classmate that became a good friend (in the early 1970s in Savannah, Georgia, it was rare for white and black teenagers to have close friendships). My friend made me something that I put on my key chain, and I kept it through junior high school, high school, and even through college. Every time I looked at my keys, I thought of my old classmate and the special relationship we had that crossed over racial boundaries.

When I mentioned his name in the sermon, one of our church members recognized the name. She knew him. She even worked with him. I couldn't believe it. I was going to reconnect with him after all these years. So, she and I set up a surprise reunion. I couldn't wait. Come the big day, my old friend entered the room. I knew he wouldn't know who I was unless I told him my name because I looked so different. After all, it had been twenty-three years since we had seen each other.

I was right. He didn't know who I was when he saw me. But what really surprised me was that he didn't know who I was even after I told him my name. He didn't remember me—at all! I couldn't understand it.

Could that happen with Mr. Mohini? Of course, it could! Maybe our relationship wasn't as significant as I thought. Maybe he was just being nice to me in order to sell clothes. After all, he had to make a living, and he was a great salesman. I had spent a lot more time with my junior high friend than I did with Mr. Mohini. If my junior-high friend didn't remember me, how would Mr. Mohini? Why put myself through that disappointment?

For peace of mind and comfort, that's why.

You see, I love downtown Savannah. No one loves walking downtown more than I do, especially along Broughton Street. But those walks were not as wonderful as they could have been because I often thought about Mr. Mohini and how I never had tried to reconnect with him.

One Sunday in early 2018, while I was greeting people after I led a worship service, my cousin Kim Johnson said to me, "Billy, did you know that the New York Boutique is still on Broughton Street?" Kim had seen the production of *Godspell* at Valdosta State—she knew the shirt story. But why, after almost forty years, would she mention the New York Boutique? Where did that come from? She didn't know that it bothered me that I never had gone back to try to see Mr. Mohini.

The very next day I was to be at a four o'clock meeting at the Chatham County Courthouse in downtown Savannah. I parked on Broughton Street and walked over to the nearby courthouse. When I arrived, I learned that the meeting had been cancelled. I walked back to my car on Broughton Street. Just before I opened the car door, I decided that enough was enough. I at least needed to try to see Mr. Mohini or try to find out what happened to him.

So, I walked to Mohini's New York Boutique. But to my surprise, to my disappointment, and maybe to my relief, the store was no longer there. A new store had moved in and taken its place.

I was confused. Kim had said that she recently had seen the store. Could it be in another location on Broughton Street? As I walked back to my car, I tried to look for the store's sign. Eureka! There it was in front of me: New York Boutique.

But then I noticed that it no longer was *Mohini's* New York Boutique, only New York Boutique. Was Mr. Mohini no longer involved? Would they even know who he was?

I opened the door and saw several young people. One of them apparently worked at the store because she asked if she could help me. After I responded to her, my eyes were drawn to a short, balding man behind the counter. He looked in my direction. Could it be? Could that be Mr. Mohini after all these years?

I started walking toward him.

"Are you Mr. Mohini?" I asked.

I didn't wait for him to say anything, because as I got closer, I could tell it was indeed Mr. Mohini. He was doing the same thing he always did before—manning the same post as he did forty years ago. I couldn't believe it!

I said, "Do you know who I am?"

He looked at me for a few seconds and said, "No, I don't."

I took a deep breath and said, "Well, about forty years

ago, when I was about nineteen or twenty…."

Before I said another word, he raised a finger, as if to cut me off or as if he had thought of something. He turned around with his back to me, still with his finger in the air, as I continued trying to explain who I was. He opened a drawer and rummaged through folders and papers for what seemed like five minutes. Then he turned around and smiled. In his hand was the picture postcard of me that I had sent him forty years ago. He had my postcard picture in the drawer with him at work for all those years.

Then, with that wonderful, familiar accent, he said, "I have heard that you are now a minister."

I was waiting for him to say, "That's too bad." Instead, he started telling me about how important his faith was to him, how every day he took time to reflect and to give thanks. That was the key, he said, for him having had a long, successful, meaningful life.

He then introduced me to his son, the son who was in India when I first met Mr. Mohini. He was in his forties and was helping run the store with his father. His son took a picture of Mr. Mohini and me. Then Mr. Mohini gave me his business card, so I had his contact information. I noticed that the word Mohini was not anywhere on the card. Come to find out, Mr. Mohini's name was not "Mohini;" it was "Mohan."

He explained how the word Mohini originated. I didn't quite grasp all that he said about it, but I know that it had something to do with his wife.

Anyway, I went back to the car and got two copies of my first book to give to Mohan and his son, so they could know a little bit about what I had been up to for the last forty years.

Mr. Mohini

How good it was to reconnect with my friend, Mohan.

How good it was to meet his son.

How good it was to be remembered.

Today, walks on Broughton Street have never been better.

STUDY QUESTIONS

- What is the first friendship you had with someone from another country?

- Have you ever had an experience like Billy had with the friend who did not remember him? What was it like? How did it feel?

- Why do we sometimes avoid getting in touch with people from our past who have been important in our lives?

- We know what the experience of seeing Mohan after many years was like for Billy. What do you think it was like for Mohan?

- Is there someone from your past that you need to get in touch with? If so, what is holding you back?

- Can you think of a time when someone from your distant past reconnected with you? What was it like? How did it feel?

- What will you remember most from this story?

SINGING AT MADISON SQUARE GARDEN

I recently read the sad news that Anne Donovan died at the age of 56 on June 13, 2018. I first heard about Anne in the 1980s. Coming out of high school, she was the most recruited female basketball player in the nation going into college. At 6'8", she was both tall and athletic.

Memories of Anne made me think of 1981, the year I moved to New York City to pursue a career in musical theatre. I did not have a job, so I applied at a temp agency. Temp agencies would send people to one of the many businesses in Manhattan that needed temporary help. A person could work at an office for a day or two—or maybe a week or two. After that job was over, the agency would send the person to another company for another temp job.

The very first place the agency sent me was the Special Events Department at Manufacturers Hanover Bank. The Special Events Department marketed the sporting events that the bank sponsored, such as the Manufacturers Hanover Westchester Golf Classic.

The person I worked for was a young woman named Mimi Senkowski. Mimi had been an excellent college athlete.

She had considered playing professional basketball but had the opportunity to take this job with Manufacturers Hanover. It was a great fit for her, as it combined sports with business.

Basically, my job was stuffing envelopes for Mimi's many projects. In fact, there were so many projects and envelopes that I ended up staying at the Special Events Department longer than most temp jobs. Within her busy schedule, Mimi took the time to get to know something about me and my dreams of being on Broadway.

One day Mimi said to me, "Billy, how would you like to sing the national anthem at Madison Square Garden?"

"Excuse me?"

She said, "You're a singer, right?"

"Yes."

"Well, we're sponsoring a basketball tournament at the Garden, and we'll need someone to sing the national anthem. Would you be interested?"

I said, "But you don't know how well I can sing. You don't know how I sound."

"Can you bring me a tape of you singing?"

"You bet," I said.

Mimi had no idea what this opportunity meant to me. I had just moved to New York and was finding it very difficult breaking into the business. Singing at the Garden not only would give me exposure, but it also would be great to have on my résumé. It could open doors for me.

Also, Mimi probably didn't know that I was a huge sports fan. The Garden is where Willis Reed made his unbelievable entrance on one leg to play in the deciding championship game against the Lakers in 1970. The Garden was the home of the first Muhammad Ali/Joe Frazier bout that was billed as The Fight of the Century. Singing the national anthem was great. But singing the national anthem at the Garden was incredible!

I brought in a tape of me singing for Mimi to listen to. Fortunately, I passed the test; and, in 1981, I went to sing at the Garden for the Women's Christmas Classic, a game that would feature some of the nation's best women college basketball players. That was where I saw the great Anne Donavan, who was playing for Old Dominion. She was warming up as I stood nervously on the side of the court waiting to be introduced for the anthem.

I wasn't nervous about singing—I was nervous about remembering the words. I had told myself that if I ever sang "The Star-Spangled Banner" at an event, I would never use a cheat sheet. A person should know the anthem by heart. But I also knew that there had been many famous singers who had messed up the anthem and had never lived it down. I could mention some names, but we need to give these people a break.

Someone gave me a signal to walk to center court, as a large, rich voice came over the PA: "Now, will you please rise for 'The Star-Spangled Banner,' sung by Mr. Billy Hester?" I was standing at center court—I was standing at center court in Madison Square Garden! The crowd got quiet, and I started the song.

Then I did something that singers are never supposed to do. I was so nervous about remembering the words that I tried to process the words in my mind far in advance as I was singing. Instead of staying in the moment, I tried thinking about the words that would be coming up after the next phrase or two. I had a terrible revelation: I could not remember some words. I totally blanked. The phrase I couldn't think of was, "And the rockets' red glare!" It's one of the easiest and most memorable parts of the song, but I had drawn a complete blank.

As I kept getting closer and closer to that part of the song, I started panicking inside. What was I going to do? It was not like forgetting words to a song in a musical. Since most people don't know all the words to a song in a musical, you can make up words if need be. But you can't make up words to the national anthem.

I couldn't believe what was about to happen. I was going to look like a fool! How would I ever live it down? This would be seen not only by all the people at the Garden, but also by all of those watching on television. It would be on tape! They would play it over and over on *SportsCenter*!

All I knew to do when I got to that part of the song was to sing the tune with the vowel sound, "Ah." At least people would hear the tune. So, when I got to that point, I opened my mouth and sang, "*Ahhhnd* the rockets' red glare!" Somehow the words came out. It was a miracle! I was so pumped up that I sang the rest of the song with great gusto. I'm sure others have sung the anthem better at the Garden, but I doubt anyone ever sang it with more excitement, passion, and gratitude.

As I walked off the court, a man came up to me and said, "Man, you did a great job! I really liked how you sang it." "Thank you very much," I said.

The man continued, "And it was great how you didn't

have to look up at the words."

I said, "Excuse me?"

"It was great how you didn't have to look up at the words."

"What do you mean?"

"You know, how they were flashing up the words for everyone on the electric signboard."

I looked up, and there was the signboard. The words had been in front of me the whole time! I went through all that anxiety for nothing.

What if I had not come up with the words? I would have gone through incredible embarrassment for no reason at all. The words had been right there all along.

I learned a lot from that experience. I now ask questions and try to become familiar with my surroundings whenever I am preaching, singing, performing, or presenting. It's a lesson that helps me every Sunday when I preach. It's a lesson that helps me every time someone in the community asks me to present something.

This experience also reminds me of the power of kindness. Mimi's thoughtfulness helped my career. Whenever I handed over my résumé to casting agents at an audition, they saw something they rarely saw. They saw something that made me stand out. Nine times out of ten, they would ask, "You really sang the national anthem at Madison Square Garden?"

And I would say, "Yep." But I didn't tell them that I almost forgot the words.

My former boss, Mimi Senkowski, would get married and become Mimi Griffin. She became a sports commentator for ESPN and CBS. In 2014, she was inducted into the Women's Basketball Hall of Fame, and she recently received the 2018 Naismith Outstanding Contributor to Basketball Award. It's great when good things happen to kind and generous people.

Thank you, Mimi, for your act of kindness and generosity. It contributed to my getting employment in theatrical productions, which led to the eventual meeting of my future wife. Four children later, your invitation to sing has reminded me again and again how one simple act of kindness can lead to amazing and unforeseeable results.

STUDY QUESTIONS

- Have you ever been to Madison Square Garden? What was the occasion?

- Have you ever been in a position where you narrowly escaped a very embarrassing situation? What happened? How did it make you feel?

- Why do you think Mimi offered Billy the opportunity to sing at the Garden?

- Who are the Mimis in your life—people who have helped you in your career?

- What specific ways can you be an encourager to others?

- Billy made a mistake by trying to think of the words of the song in advance instead of staying in the moment. How can that relate to how you live your life?

- What will you remember most from this story?

LEARNING A SAVANNAH ACCENT

A round 1984, I was in my New York apartment on 29th Street when I got a phone call like I never had gotten before.

"Hello?"

"Is this Billy Hester?

"Yes, it is."

"Hi, Billy. My name is Bill Sadler. You don't know me, but I'm a fellow actor. I recently was cast in Neil Simon's play *Biloxi Blues*, which will be coming to Broadway. The character I am playing is supposed to be from Savannah, Georgia. I have heard that you're from Savannah. Is that right?"

"Yes, I am."

"I would like to learn a Savannah accent, so I can portray the character more authentically. I know this may sound a little strange, but would it be okay with you if I came over to your place and listened to you talk?" (When's the last time a stranger has asked to listen to you talk?)

The actor said, "I really would like to hear a Savannah dialect."

"Sure," I said, "that would be fine."

Learning a Savannah Accent

I gave Bill my address, and he came over so I could speak my best "Savannah" for him. He was playing the role of Sergeant Merwin J. Toomey. You can tell that it's a wonderful role just by the name of the character. He is a major player in the play.

I told Bill that I wished he could hear my high school football coach, Doyle Kelley. Doyle would give him quite a dialect to emulate. In fact, Bill could copy Doyle's total persona, because Doyle was a whole lot like Sergeant Toomey. But that's another story for another book.

I wish I could have seen Bill's interpretation of the character, but I never got to see the show. I *have* seen the movie, however. Three years after *Biloxi Blues* opened on Broadway in 1985, the play was made into a film. Actor Christopher Walken played Sergeant Toomey. The film has a wonderful script. "It preaches," as we ministers like to say. I often have used lines from the film in sermons because the story offers a bounty of moral and spiritual lessons.

Arnold Epstein, a private in basic training under Toomey, says one of my favorite lines. The scrawny, philosophical, and awkward Epstein tells his sergeant, "I just don't think it's necessary to dehumanize a man in order to get him to perform. You can get better results raising our spirits than lowering our dignity."

Another one of my favorite scenes is between Epstein and the main character, Eugene Jerome, who hopes to be a writer and who is always journaling in a book. Jerome says to Epstein, "Why is it that we come from the same place, but I can't understand you?"

Epstein replies, "You're a witness. You're always

standing around watching what's happening, scribbling in your book what other people do. You have to get in the middle of it. You have to take sides. Make a contribution to the fight."

"What fight?" says Eugene.

"Any fight," says Arnold. "One you believe in. Until you do, you'll never be a writer."

❦

Bill Sadler performed in *Biloxi Blues* on Broadway for over a year. As I recall, the review in the *New York Times* said that his Savannah accent was outstanding. The show won the Tony Award for Best Play, and Bill was nominated for a Drama Desk Award for Outstanding Featured Actor in a Play.

Who in the world tracks down someone they don't know, just so they can hear him talk? Who goes to the trouble of finding someone from Savannah when probably just any old southern accent would work for the character? Who goes to that trouble? Who works on those kinds of details?

Bill Sadler.

❦

I've never seen Bill again since that night—in person, that is. I have seen him on television and on the silver screen countless times. In fact, I'm sure you have too; for Bill has done very well with his acting career. He has starred in *The Shawshank Redemption*, *The Green Mile*, *Die Hard 2*, *Iron Man 3*, *August Rush*, among many other films. He's also been featured on a "zillion" television shows.

Bill's success doesn't surprise me. It shouldn't surprise anyone that a person who is so dedicated to his craft that he would track down a stranger with a Savannah accent would become very successful.

Sage Arnold Epstein would be proud of Bill because Bill has not been a witness. Bill has gotten in the middle of it and has given it his all.

May we all get off the sidelines and make a contribution to the fight. May we give our all to pursuing our dreams and our passions.

STUDY QUESTIONS

- What kind of accent do you have? Is it regional? From your parents? Do you like it?

- What, if anything, does Bill Sadler's attention to detail and going the extra mile have to do with his successful career?

- In the play, Bill portrayed an alpha male who could be controlling and extremely hard on others. How do you respond to such people in your life?

- Can you share any examples of when people have gotten better results by raising people's spirits rather than lowering their dignity?

- Epstein encourages his friend to put down his pencil and contribute to the fight. What does he mean?

- Are you contributing to any fights?

- What will you remember most from this story?

A SPECIAL TRIP TO VALDOSTA

I n 1978, when I was in college at Valdosta State, I was in a wonderful production of *The Lion in Winter*, a play that revolves around the tumultuous, passionate, and political relationship between King Henry II of England and his wife, Eleanor of Aquitaine. If you are not familiar with this part of history, Henry had Eleanor imprisoned after she had borne him eight children. She was in prison for sixteen years until Henry's death.

In our production, the roles of Henry and Eleanor were played by two excellent actors named Mack Anthony and Ellyn Eaves. I played their troubled son John.

In 2018, I was pleasantly surprised to receive an email from Eleanor of Aquitaine (Ellyn Eaves). She said that she was now "out of prison" and was coming to Savannah. Ellyn had married and was now Ellyn Eaves-Hileman and was living in Rhode Island. Unfortunately, I was going to be out of town while she was visiting Savannah. But I made it back just in time to have breakfast with her on the day she left. It was so good seeing my college friend and theatrical "mom."

The day after I had breakfast with my friend of thirty-nine years, I got a message from another longtime friend, a woman named Aleen Melton. I had known Mrs. Melton even longer than Ellyn. Mrs. Melton helped raise me at my childhood church. Her message conveyed that she was recently cleaning and going through some files, where she found the program from a play she saw me in during college. She wondered if I wanted the program.

This took me by surprise because I didn't remember Mrs. Melton coming to see me in a play in college. It's a three-and-a-half-hour drive from Savannah to Valdosta.

I called her back. "Mrs. Melton. I heard that you found a program from one of the shows I did in college. You came to see me in a show in Valdosta?"

She said, "Yes, a little group of us from the church came. There were at least eight of us that made the trip."

I said, "What show was it?"

She said, "*The Lion in Winter*."

"That's so strange," I said. "Just yesterday, I had breakfast with the woman who had the lead role in that show. That's incredible."

So, I had breakfast with Ellyn with whom I did *The Lion in Winter* thirty-nine years ago, and the next day Mrs. Melton gave me the thirty-nine-year-old program from the show. Wow!

But that is not the most unbelievable part of the story. The most unbelievable part is that at least eight non-family members—eight adults from my childhood church—drove three and a half hours to Valdosta, Georgia, to see me in a college play. And I didn't even have the lead role.

A Special Trip to Valdosta

Now, it's not like this group of people was going to New York or to Atlanta to see me in a show. It's not like they could say, "Let's go to the Empire State Building and see New York while we go catch Billy's show." It's not like they could say, "Let's go see Billy's show, and we can see something else at the Fox Theatre while we're there in Atlanta."

No, they came to Valdosta, Georgia. There was no other reason to go to Valdosta. Valdosta now has something called "Wild Adventures," an amusement park. But Valdosta didn't have it back in the 1970s.

Valdosta probably had a Stuckey's, but I don't think they said,"Hey y'all, why don't we drive down to see Billy in a play in Valdosta? And we can pick up some Pecan Log Rolls while we're there!"

I had not remembered that this group of people made this trip to see me in the show. But, after I had the conversation with Mrs. Melton, I vaguely remember it happening.

There are many other things that those people—and other people at my childhood church—did for me while I was growing up that I have forgotten. But what I have never forgotten was feeling incredibly loved by the members of my church family.

I have forgotten many of the specific events. I have forgotten kind and loving things they *said* to me. I have forgotten kind and loving things they *did* for me. However, I remember how they made me *feel*. The things they said and did helped me feel loved, helped me feel important, helped me feel valued. And I have never forgotten that feeling.

It was that feeling that helped me go off to college. It was that feeling that helped me move to New York to pursue a career in theatre. It was that feeling that helped me dive into seminary and into the ministry. That feeling came from members of my church family who constantly expressed love and encouragement to me.

Human beings are not independent. We were made to be interdependent. We were conceived and formed in the body of another, held and fed and cared for in our infancy and childhood. We weren't made to be independent physically, emotionally, or spiritually.

We make it through life and thrive in life based on our networks, communities, neighbors, families, friends, and colleagues. Humans need communities to live, even as we find ourselves increasingly isolated and caught up in a world of rampant individualism that threatens to undermine all the messages the Bible has sought to teach us about how to relate to one another.

It dawned on me that those eight or more people who drove three and a half hours to see me in a show thirty-nine years ago didn't do it just for me. It was an incredible thing they did, a tremendous gift; however, they also did it for themselves because the people on that trip were dear, dear friends.

You see, if the Meltons went on a trip to Valdosta with a group, I can tell you who the other people were. If the Meltons went, then the Simmerlys had to be one of the other couples and the Holloways and the Richardsons and the Brewtons. They were the closest of friends.

They had been there for one another through the death of their loved ones. They had been there for one another when one of them almost died in a car accident. They had been there for one another when someone had to stay in the hospital for a long time. They helped raised one another's children. They all loved to laugh and have a good time together. These people came to love and care for one another—would do anything for one another. They loved to spend time together. They loved me too, but the trip to Valdosta was, more or less, an excuse for them to be together, for them to be the Church, the Body of Christ.

The Lion in Winter is a play about a dysfunctional family whose members treated one another with great disdain. A special group of people from Savannah viewed the production in Valdosta—people who were not blood-related, but who treated one another like a real family.

STUDY QUESTIONS

- Other than a wedding, graduation, or funeral, have you traveled over three hours to support a friend in an event? What was the situation?

- What's the difference between being independent and being interdependent?

- Is anyone truly independent?

- From what sources do you receive love and encouragement?

- What communities, groups, or networks of support do you have?

- What keeps people from being part of a support group?

- What can you do to encourage those who don't have a group?

- What will you remember most from this story?

HELPING PEOPLE SMILE

I f you stay up late at night watching television, you may come upon an infomercial about Supersmile toothpaste. Supersmile was invented by a dentist named Irwin Smigel, who was dubbed "The Father of Aesthetic Dentistry." Every time I see that infomercial, I think of the interesting experience I had with Dr. Smigel on television!

I was a Tetracycline baby. Tetracycline was a drug that was given to some pregnant women in the 1950s. Later, it was discovered that the drug darkened many of their children's teeth. I was one of those children. I, of course, wished my teeth were whiter, especially since I was in the acting profession.

I also had other issues with my teeth. During a high school football practice, the chinstrap on my helmet broke; and my helmet came off when another player's helmet struck me in the face. As one can imagine, this collision caused several tooth issues. Due to this accident, I had to wear braces on my teeth for a total of six years. None of my classmates in junior high school or high school ever saw me without braces on my teeth.

When I moved to New York, my mother read an article about Dr. Smigel, who was one of the first dentists to start using bonding. He had brightened the teeth of Elizabeth Taylor, Martha Graham, Tony Bennett, and Bruce Willis. "The eyes may be the soul of the face, but the mouth is the first thing people look at," Dr. Smigel told *New York* magazine in 1981. "Now, bonding has given us the possibility of instant transformation, since it can be done in a matter of hours, not days or years." Then he added, "Nothing will have the emotional impact on the public that bonding will have."

In 1981, after my mother dipped greatly into her savings, she arranged for me to see Dr. Smigel. I found myself sitting in a dental chair in his Manhattan office on Madison Avenue. While his hands were in my mouth, an assistant came to him and said, "Dr. Smigel, you've got an important phone call." After he excused himself to take the call, he came back to me and said (in his soft, husky voice that sounded similar to Marlon Brando in *The Godfather*), "Billy, how would you like to go on television with me?"

That sounded like an offer I couldn't refuse. It was an offer I didn't *want* to refuse. I had just arrived in New York to pursue an acting career and needed all the exposure I could get.

Dr. Smigel explained, "I just got a call from *The Regis Philbin Show*. I want to show the world the new dental technique that I currently am using on you. How about I finish all your teeth except one. We'll leave that one tooth undone, so I can do it on the show." Here I was, fairly new to New York; and I was already going to meet Regis and be on his show. How wonderful!

On the day of the shooting, Dr. Smigel, his wife, their daughter, my sister, and I rode in a chauffeured limousine to the studio. We walked in, and it suddenly dawned on me that Regis' show was in front of a live studio audience. Dr. Smigel was going to work on me, right in front of people. I'd be drooling and spitting in front of them. But, hey, such is show biz, right?

So, there I was, with Dr. Smigel working on me in a makeshift dental chair. I was dribbling, drooling, and expectorating in front of everyone. Then Dr. Smigel threw about sixteen cotton balls into my mouth. Now, I *looked* like the Godfather.

While Dr. Smigel was working on me, Regis asked him questions about the product and the procedure. Then, being the great host that he is, Regis gestured to me and said, "And Irwin, who do we have here?"

Alright, this was my big moment! I was hoping to say something like, "Hi, I'm Billy Hester, a budding young actor from Savannah, Georgia!" But I had all those cotton balls in my mouth, so I couldn't talk! Not only that, Dr. Smigel's fingers were down my throat. So, unfortunately, I couldn't say anything.

Dr. Smigel was caught off guard. As he tried to introduce me, he got flustered. Granted, he was trying to work on me and be interviewed at the same time. He said, "Oh yes, yes— this is one of my patients. This is Billy, Billy, Billy Casper!"

(Billy Casper? Billy Casper? Billy Casper was a professional golfer in the 1960s!)

I wasn't about to go through all of this and have people

think that I was Billy Casper. Even with a hundred cotton balls in my mouth and Dr. Smigel's hands down my throat, I tried my best to get out the words, "No, no. Billy HESTER! Billy HESTER!" It was quite a comedy skit. We laughed about it after the show as the Smigels were gracious enough to take my sister and me out to a nice dinner.

That night, my new teeth with my new smile were on display. I attended the performance of a Broadway show, *Brighton Beach Memoirs*. At intermission, a woman came up to me and said, "Weren't you on *The Regis Philbin Show* today?" I couldn't believe someone recognized me. My head had been tilted back the entire time, Dr. Smigel had been hovering over me, and the stack of cotton balls in my mouth made me look like a chipmunk. This woman had to have an incredible eye to recognize me under those circumstances.

I said, "Yes, that was me spitting and drooling."

"By the way," she said, "your teeth look wonderful!"

"Thank you," I said. She had no idea how much her words meant to me. She did not know the struggle I had had with my teeth my entire life. How good it was to be able to smile with confidence.

After seeing one of Dr. Smigel's infomercials a couple of years ago, I decided to try to reconnect with him. I didn't have his email address, but I sent him a message through a business email address, not knowing if the email would reach him. To my surprise, he sent me a very thoughtful email the very next day.

I wish I had saved his email because I recently learned that the master dentist died in 2016. His death must have been just after we had reconnected.

Thanks, Doc, for helping me smile, and thank you for the many smiles you put on other people. I look forward to our good reunion in eternity. In the meantime, say "Hello" to Billy Casper for me.

STUDY QUESTIONS

- What would you have done if you were in Billy's situation (packed with cotton balls) and Dr. Smigel introduced you incorrectly on television?

- Dr. Smigel dedicated his life to helping people have a good smile. What difference does it make if a salesperson, bank teller, cashier, or some other acquaintance smiles at you? How does it make you feel?

- There's an old saying, "Smile and the whole world smiles with you." Does that proverb ring true to you? If it does, why do you think it is so?

- Someone once said, "Everyone smiles in the same language." What do you think?

- What made you smile today?

- What can you do in your life to smile more?

- What will you remember most from this story?

A Little Help from My Friends

I recently had the remote control and was channel surfing when I came upon a familiar face. It was the very distinctive face of a college classmate of mine named Ray McKinnon. Ray and I had been theatre majors together at Valdosta State College in South Georgia. We graduated the same year, 1981. Ray was from the very small town of Adel, Georgia. He was a great guy, fun to be around, and a very good actor. One play where I especially enjoyed acting with Ray was *Bus Stop* by William Inge.

The reason I saw Ray on television was because I had turned to a channel that was showing the movie *The Blind Side*. *The Blind Side* was very successful and earned an Academy Award nomination for Best Film in 2010. The movie is based on the life of professional football player Michael Oher. Michael was one of twelve children born to a mother who was addicted to alcohol, crack, and cocaine. His father, who Michael barely knew, died in prison. Michael grew up in the projects in Memphis, and eventually became homeless. He attended eleven different schools his first nine years as a student.

During his high school years, a white family, the Tuohys,

took Michael, who is African-American, into their home and eventually adopted him. One of the things I like about the film is that you not only see how the love and care offered by the Tuohys transforms Michael, but you also see how Michael's presence transforms the Tuohy family. It's a beautiful film about how we all need one another and how we can do great things with a little help from our friends.

In many ways, the film is a psychological and emotional drama. Since Michael happens to be a really good and successful athlete, the film's dressing is football. And guess who played Michael's high school coach? Ray McKinnon.

After graduating from Valdosta State, the boy from the small town of Adel moved to Atlanta. He found himself getting cast in the film *Driving Miss Daisy*, along with the television shows *In the Heat of the Night* and *Matlock*. Then came blockbuster films like *Apollo 13* and *O Brother, Where Art Thou?* He also had a recurring role as Rev. H. W. Smith in the HBO *Deadwood* series. Then, in 2001, Ray wrote, directed, and starred in a short film called *The Accountant*. Incredibly, Ray's film won an Oscar for Best Live Action Short Film at the Academy Awards in 2002.

But this story is not so much about Ray McKinnon or Michael Oher. This story is *really* about a fellow named Joel Boatright, who was one of Ray's professors in college. For, you see, Michael Oher was not the only person who needed a little help from his friends to make it. Michael's coach in the film, Ray McKinnon, needed a little help too. But first, back to Joel.

Joel Boatright was the cool tech professor in the Theatre

Department at Valdosta State College. He was a natural craftsman. He must have come out of the womb wearing a tool belt. Visually, he was a mixture of Elvis, James Dean, and Wolfman Jack. His mode of transportation was either a motorcycle or a pickup truck. He was one of those professors you felt comfortable calling by his first name. He was the professor you would go off campus with for lunch to grab a hoagie. He was the professor you could talk over your problems with or tell jokes with.

Joel's personality changed, however, when you took his classes. Theatre majors dreaded taking them. Many students become theatre majors to perform, to be on stage. Joel taught the technical classes: set design, lighting design, and set construction. He did not care if your forte was acting, singing, or dancing. He still demanded excellence from you. Most of our GPAs went down when we took one of Joel's classes. If your work wasn't done to perfection, he would fail you in a heartbeat. Joel had the incredible ability to accept our humanity and faults while at the same time demand our excellence.

I can remember Joel taking me into the huge theatre workshop for the first time my freshman year. The workshop was where the sets were built to help create the magic on stage. Items that were foreign to me filled the large space: saws, boards, ladders, paint, tools. I'm sure that it quickly became clear to Joel that I was not in my element. I couldn't nail two boards together without making mincemeat of a thumb. But Joel ignored my construction disabilities and acted like I could do anything. In fact, he expected me to do anything. So, I had to stretch and do things I didn't think I could do.

I can't say that I'm a jack of all trades. In fact, people laugh when they think of me trying to fix or repair things. But I can say that I made it through four years of college with Joel Boatright as my theatre tech professor, and that is saying a lot!

❦

During his thirty years teaching at Valdosta State, Joel built many close relationships. When he retired, I was among many students who drove to Valdosta for his retirement party. Ray McKinnon was not able to be there—he was probably shooting a film! But Ray made sure to send a letter to be read to all of those in attendance. In his letter, Ray expressed the great significance Joel had played in his life. I already had known that Ray and Joel had a special relationship. What I didn't know until the reading of Ray's letter was that there was an occasion when Joel had to get Ray out of jail. I also learned that there were other students Joel had rescued from jail. The man who would flunk you in a second for not reaching your potential would do anything for you if you were in trouble.

❦

In 2014, almost thirty years later, I directed a production of the musical *Cotton Patch Gospel*. At one of our performances, someone encouraged me to peep from behind backstage to see who was sitting on the front row. I looked and saw a man who looked like a silver-haired Elvis, James Dean, and Wolfman Jack. It was Joel! My old theatre professor was sitting on the front row with his wife, Monie!

I learned that the surprise visit was arranged by Joel and

one of our church members, Grady Mills. Grady is a retired United Methodist minister who also had been a theatre major at Valdosta State. In fact, Grady and Joel had been theatre majors together. I had not realized that Joel had been a student at Valdosta State before being a professor. Joel and Grady had become close friends. They even were in each other's weddings.

When Grady told Joel that I was a minister at a church in Savannah and that I was directing the play, they planned the surprise. What a wonderful gift it was for me to have Joel and Monie there and to reconnect with them!

Speaking of gifts, we happened to have a door prize during the run of the show for the person who came the closest to guessing the number of cheese balls that were in a huge, clear container. At the end of the two-week run, Joel had come the closest. The correct number of cheese balls was 1,335; Joel had guessed 1,330. I wondered if Joel had pulled out the measuring tape he always had attached to his belt and made measurements to determine his estimation. He couldn't believe he won. When we gave him his prize, he said it was the first time he had ever won anything.

Unfortunately, four months later, the 71-year-old Joel died while cutting large, rotten limbs off trees at his son's house. Though many of us were in shock when we learned of the death of our friend and professor, we took comfort in the fact that Joel died while working with nature and in the great outdoors that he loved so much.

Joel's former students, friends, and family members did a tremendous job of honoring Joel at his funeral. They remembered well the teacher who would do anything for you while also demanding your best efforts.

Where would we be without people in our lives who are willing to help us? Where would we be, especially, without those we call teacher or professor?

Here's to those underpaid, dedicated souls who seek to give us the tools to pursue our dreams and goals.

STUDY QUESTIONS

- Metaphorically, are you more comfortable being on stage or working behind the scenes? Why?

- What teachers or coaches have played a significant role in your life? What did they do to impact your life?

- Can you pinpoint one particular thing that someone has done for you that greatly impacted your life or made life better for you? Or have you mostly been helped in a lot of smaller ways by different people? Or is it maybe both?

- Why is it challenging to find people who accept our faults while at the same time demand our excellence?

- How are you at accepting the faults of your friends while also holding them accountable?

- What will you remember most from this story?

WHAT OTIS REDDING GAVE ME FOR CHRISTMAS

E veryone knows that Christmas can be a difficult time for people. Ministers are not immune to the holiday blues. Even though we try to get our congregations excited and prepared for Christmas, we are just as susceptible as they are to having periods of depression during the holidays. Such was the case for me several years ago.

I'm not sure what had me so despondent. For one thing, the weather was extremely warm for late November. It surely didn't seem like it was time for chestnuts roasting on an open fire. Everyone in Savannah was roasting.

I also was frustrated with the commercialism of the season. Besides the stores selling Christmas items the day after Halloween, some radio stations started playing Christmas music twenty-four hours a day, seven days a week in early November! What happened to Advent? What happened to preparing our hearts and minds for Christmas?

But there were deeper reasons for my depression. Most of them had to do with what was going on in the world. Theologian Karl Barth famously said that we should "read the Bible in one hand and the newspaper in the other." It is important to know what's going in the world if we are to be instruments of peace and social justice. But with the Internet and social media, it's easy to get burned out from hearing about all the chaos, destruction, and divisiveness in the world.

Also contributing to my downcast spirit was the fact that our house was infested with little flying critters. The infestation called for a special trip to Walmart for a can of bug spray.

After searching for the special brand of spray for our special bugs, I finally located it in aisle 19b and got in line to pay for it. As I was waiting in line with my can of bug spray, I wondered how I could get in the Christmas spirit. I looked to my right, and there stood a rack of Christmas CDs. At that time of year, every store had a rack of Christmas CDs by the cash register for $3.99. My first thought was, "Oh no, not more Christmas music." But then I wondered if there was a CD of Christmas music I had never heard—something new, something fresh, something that would give me some life.

I got out of line, walked over to the rack, and started browsing through the CDs. Most of them consisted of traditional music and artists you typically see at this time of year. But then my eyes locked onto two CDs I had never seen before.

One was the *Jethro Tull Christmas Album* (I didn't know Jethro Tull had a Christmas album.). I thought, "Well, this has got to be different." And it was. If you like flute music, you need to get the *Jethro Tull Christmas Album*. But it didn't quite do the trick for me.

The other CD I bought was called *Christmas Soul*. It consisted of a variety of African-American artists singing traditional Christmas songs. For instance, there was a version of "I Saw Mommy Kissing Santa Claus" by The Impressions. It had a lot of giddy-up to it and fabulous harmonies. But the song I liked the most—the one I needed to hear—was a version of "White Christmas," sung by the great Otis Redding.

Otis sang the song with incredible soul and passion. I had never heard "White Christmas" sung this way before. As I listened to it, I found myself thinking, "Otis, I need what you have. Otis, I am numb. Give me some of your spirit. Give me some of your passion."

In the recording, Otis was crying out for a white Christmas—he was begging for it to happen. You could tell he was hurting and wanted something to lift him up. As I listened to the song, I thought, "I know what you mean, Otis. I feel the same way. I need something to lift me up, too!"

❦

Otis Redding was born in Dawson Georgia, the son of a Baptist minister. If you're the son of a Baptist minister in Georgia, you sing in the choir. And Otis did. In the 1960s, he became a very popular vocalist and songwriter (he wrote the wonderful song "Respect," sung by the late Aretha Franklin). But Otis was mostly known as a vocalist, and some regard him as the greatest male soul singer of all time.

In 1966, he was voted the Best International Male Vocalist of the Year, an award that had gone to Elvis Presley for ten straight years. He recorded his most famous song, "Sittin' On the Dock of the Bay," on December 7, 1967. Just three days later, on December 10th, Otis died in an airplane crash at the young age of twenty-six.

But Otis' music and legacy are still strong today. His ongoing popularity is largely due to his uncanny ability to sing with great passion and feeling — with soul.

Soul music is a combination of gospel music and rhythm-and-blues. There's soul music that expresses great joy and happiness, and there's soul music that expresses great sorrow and sadness. Soul Music is very much like the psalms (songs) in the Bible.

There are psalms that express great joy and happiness, called "Psalms of Thanksgiving" or "Psalms of Praise." A good example is: "Make a joyful noise to the Lord, all the earth. Worship the Lord with gladness; come into God's presence with singing" (Psalm 100:1-2).

But there are other psalms in the Bible called "laments." The laments express sorrow and sadness, fear and anxiety. A good example is: "How long, O Lord? Will you forget me forever? How long will you hide your face from me?" (Psalm 13:1).

I didn't realize that it was okay to speak to God so honestly until I discovered the psalms of laments while I was in seminary. I thought it was wrong to complain or question or doubt. But the psalmists knew that the atheist may complain, but the believer can protest. The believer can get angry and cry out, "Why?" because he or she believes there is someone to cry out to. Our protests and our questions end up being affirmations of faith.

When Otis sang "I'm dreaming of a white Christmas," he was not dreaming just about white snow on the ground on a December day. He was dreaming of something more. He was yearning for better times. For Otis, a white Christmas was a metaphor. He was dreaming of people getting along. He was dreaming of a time when people are not homeless or hungry or in pain. He was yearning for the Kingdom of God.

When I heard Otis express his feelings, it helped me get in touch with my feelings of frustration and longing—my longing for God's presence—longing for things to be better. Somehow, through expressing these feelings openly and honestly, I felt better. It wasn't a fast, upbeat, happy song that I needed to lift my spirits. I needed a *soul* song. I needed a song that helped me express my pain, my frustration, and my longing.

❦

On a Sunday during Advent season, I invite the congregation to the altar for prayer at the end of the worship service. As they come and pray, we play Otis' version of "White Christmas." It is one of our most important and moving services of the year. But you don't have to wait to do this in a community worship service. You can do it in your home or in a garden, wherever you would like Otis to help you get in touch with your feelings.

I hope you will have the kind of experience that I have had numerous times listening to Otis sing this song. I hope that, as you express your feelings to God openly and honestly, you will feel better—you will feel cleansed—so that eventually you will be able to move from singing a lament to singing a song of praise.

STUDY QUESTIONS

- Have you ever had the Christmas blues? If so, do you know why?

- Are there things you do that help when you get the blues? If so, what are they?

- Is there an artist or style of music that helps you get out of your funk?

- Some say that depression is anger turned inward. Do you agree? Why?

- Are you familiar with the laments in the Book of Psalms? Why do you think they usually end on a positive note?

- Are you comfortable expressing feelings of anger or frustration to God?

- What will you remember most from this story?

RALPH

From 1988 to 1991, I worked as an associate minister at Marble Collegiate Church on the corner of Fifth Avenue and 29th Street in New York City. One of my jobs was to meet with people who came in off the street and wanted to see a minister. Many of the people I met with were homeless.

Sadly, the majority of them came to the church for money because they had a drug or alcohol addiction. Sometimes, I would receive people's anger if they did not receive money. It was not an easy job. Instead of having a positive attitude toward such experiences, I often would go into them wishing I were somewhere else.

One day, the receptionist called me to let me know that a man had come to the church and asked to see a minister. She whispered on the phone, "I think he is a little tipsy." I went downstairs and met a homeless man named Ralph. It was pretty obvious that Ralph had a problem with alcohol. By his appearance and aroma, he had lived on the street for a long time.

Ralph spoke with a Southern accent, but it wasn't a

132

typical Southern accent. He sounded a lot like one of my cousins who had a Geechee dialect. Geechee, a name derived from the Ogeechee River near Savannah, Georgia, is a dialect known to be used by people from Savannah and the immediate Southeast coast. I asked Ralph where he was from. I almost fell out of my chair when he said, "Savannah, Georgia."

Now you need to understand that we had people come to the church who would try all kinds of tricks on me. People would come in one day with one identity and then the following week dress up in a disguise pretending to be someone else, all for the purpose of getting money. I had worked as an actor before I went into the ministry, and many of the people I met with were better performers than some of the professionals I had worked with in theatre.

When Ralph told me he was from Savannah, my first reaction was, "Oh, this guy's good. He somehow found out that I'm from Savannah, and he's pretending to be from Savannah to soften me up." I asked Ralph some Savannah questions. To my surprise, he knew the answers. In fact, he knew more about Savannah than I did.

I told Ralph that I was from Savannah too. He couldn't believe it. His eyes lit up. "How about that! How did a boy from Savannah become a minister at Marble 'Colgate' Church in New York City?" (Ralph always called Marble Collegiate Church, "Marble 'Colgate' Church." I never knew if he didn't realize that he had the wrong word or if it was the alcohol talking.)

Ralph and I started reminiscing about Savannah — talking about Benedictine, Savannah High School, the Saint Patrick's

Day Parade; you name it. Ralph had been in New York for many years, but it was clear where his roots were.

Ralph would come by the church periodically. He'd always ask for money, and I always told him that I couldn't give him any — that was a tough part of our time together. But he and I would always spend time talking about Savannah. Ralph was by far my favorite surprise guest.

❦

The spring of 1991 was a transition time for Cheri and me. We had just had our first child, and we would be moving to Savannah after having lived in the New York area for ten years.

My first job in Savannah was as the associate minister at Wesley Monumental UMC. After two years at Wesley Monumental, I was appointed to two churches: Wesley Oak UMC and Asbury Memorial UMC. My family and I moved into Wesley Oak's parsonage, which was in a section of Savannah that was an old fishing village named Thunderbolt.

I had been serving both churches for four years when, in 1997, our doorbell rang. I opened the door, and there standing on my front porch was Ralph. I couldn't believe it. Somehow he got back to Savannah and tracked me down.

It was good to see Ralph, but he did not look well. Due to his homelessness and way of living, Ralph never looked healthy. But he looked much worse. He said that he had been in pain and that he might go to the hospital. I invited Ralph into the house to talk. He asked if I could help him with some food and if I could give him a ride to where he was staying.

I asked him where he would like for me to take him to eat. "Krystals," he said. I knew it wasn't a healthy meal for him, but, by the way Ralph looked, I thought it might be one of his last meals. If the man wanted Krystals, I was going to take him to Krystal's. So off we went. After he got his order, I dropped him off at a location where he said he was staying temporarily.

After that night, I never saw Ralph again. I thought he may have died. I knew that, if Ralph was alive, I would have heard from him. He would have needed help. He would have needed money or food.

❦

Ten years later, on Thanksgiving Day, November 22, 2007, Cheri, the kids, and I joined family and friends at my Uncle Phil and Aunt Bette's house for a Thanksgiving feast. When we got home late that night, the light on our answering machine was blinking. I pushed the Play button to listen to the message:

"Billy, it's Ralph. You know, from Marble 'Colgate' Church. I just wanted to wish you a Happy Thanksgiving." He left a phone number and asked me to call him.

I couldn't believe it. Ralph was alive! And he actually sounded good.

I knew that he probably got in touch with me because he needed help. I knew he was going to ask me for money. But I was so happy to hear from him. I was so thankful that he was alive. I thought I would never see Ralph again this side of heaven, so I called him the next day.

"Ralph?"

"Yes?"

"It's Billy Hester, Rev. Hester."

"Oh, Billy! Thanks for calling back!"

"How are you doing, Ralph?"

"I'm actually doing pretty good."

"That's good. That's good. It's great to hear from you."

"Well, I was just calling you to wish you a Happy Thanksgiving."

(I was wondering what was coming next—I was waiting for the money question.)

Ralph continued, "I really do appreciate what you did for me in New York and here, and I wanted to say thank you on Thanksgiving."

"Well thank you, Ralph."

"Are you still at that church on Henry Street?"

"Yes, I am."

"Well, maybe one day I'll make it to one of your services."

"That would be great, Ralph. You do that."

"Well thanks for calling me back, Billy. Goodbye."

And he hung up the phone.

That was it. All he wanted was to thank me on Thanksgiving Day.

I have not heard from or seen Ralph since. It's been eleven years. There is a good chance that Ralph has died.

Then again, there's a good chance that he may show up on my porch one day.

And there's also a chance that he is back in New York City, blessing another young minister at Marble "Colgate" Church.

STUDY QUESTIONS

- What is your personal policy about giving money to homeless people who approach you on the street: You always give money to them; you never give money to them; or you sometimes give money to them? Why?

- Have you ever been part of a poverty simulation? If so, what did you learn from it? How did it make you feel?

- How would your life change if you lost your home? How would you spend your time if you became homeless?

- If you had been in Billy's shoes and met a homeless person with an addiction and also discovered that they were from your hometown, would you treat them any differently? Why?

- Have you ever developed a close relationship with a person who was homeless?

- What can be done in your community for someone who is homeless?

- What can be done in your community for someone who is homeless and has a drug or alcohol addiction?

- What will you remember most from this story?

THE DRIVE TO NEW JERSEY

When my wife, Cheri, and I were engaged, she lived in Manhattan; and I lived in Queens, the borough east of Manhattan. One night during this engagement period, Cheri and I had a disagreement over the telephone that turned into a doozy of an argument. I don't remember what it was about, but I remember that it was serious, so serious that it threatened the future of our relationship.

I was so distraught about our conversation that I couldn't sleep. I needed to talk to someone, but it was two o'clock in the morning. The person I especially wanted to talk with was a man named Jerry Everley. Jerry was an associate minister at Marble Collegiate Church in Manhattan. He and his wife, Carolyn, were close friends of ours. Cheri and I would sometimes baby-sit their two sons. But Jerry and Carolyn lived in Glen Rock, New Jersey, which was forty minutes west of Manhattan. Plus, it was two o'clock in the morning.

Since I was so distraught and couldn't sleep, I took an unusual course of action. I decided that I would get in my car, drive to Glen Rock, and park in front of the Everleys' house until I could see them in the morning. I know that sounds like I was feeling desperate. I was. I also knew that both Jerry and Carolyn were the kind of people who would understand.

Being in Queens, I would need to drive over the Queensboro Bridge (sometimes called the 59th Street Bridge) into Manhattan. Then I would get on 57th Street and drive from the east side of Manhattan to the west side. Then I would turn left and take Ninth Avenue downtown to go through the Lincoln Tunnel to New Jersey. I would drive the forty minutes to Glen Rock. Then, when the Everleys woke up, I would knock on their door and say, "Surprise! Need to talk!"

So, I got into my little, green Mazda 626 and drove across the 59th Street Bridge into Manhattan. Since it was two in the morning, there was very little traffic. After I crossed the bridge, I drove to 57th Street so I could drive to the west side of the City.

When I reached Seventh Avenue, I caught a red light. There was one car ahead of me. When the light turned green, the car in front started to go through the intersection. I put my foot on the gas pedal to start moving also. From out of nowhere, an 18-wheeler flew through the stop light on Seventh Avenue at highway speed, crashing into the car in front of me. The massive truck pushed the car about twenty-five yards, where it wrapped around a pole like a pretzel.

I was in shock. I stared out in front of me, until I refocused on the crushed car. I knew the passengers had to be seriously injured, if not dead.

The truck had struck the car on its right side. The force of the impact knocked out the driver's window glass, and he could not open the door. Miraculously, he climbed out of the car through the window opening. He looked to be a rather athletic young man who, somehow, still was walking. Thankfully, he had been the only person in the car. Anyone on the passenger side would not have survived.

The man's car was one of those large, old automobiles that were built like a tank. Even though the car would never be on the road again and even though it looked like a crumpled-up piece of tin, the size and solidity of the car helped save the man's life.

Since the police constantly patrol the streets of Manhattan, police cars and medical ambulances were on the scene instantly. After they arrived, I started back on my journey to the Everleys' house.

The entire time I was driving to New Jersey, I kept thinking about the accident. What if the car had not been in front of me and I had been the first car at the stoplight? If the truck had struck my small, paper-thin Mazda 626, I would not have been crawling out of it. I most likely would not be around to argue with Cheri anymore.

I kept thinking about how close I came to never seeing Cheri again and how bad it would have been for our last words to have been words of anger and hurt. Ironically, the accident happened a block from Cheri's apartment. Cheri lived on West 56th Street and Eighth Avenue. The crash was on the corner of West 57th and Seventh Avenue. If the car had not been in front of me, Cheri would have awakened to find out that I had died in a car accident almost right in front of her apartment.

When I got to the Everleys' house, I parked the car and

sat in it for about twenty minutes. Then I realized that I didn't need to talk to Jerry anymore. What I had just experienced made the disagreement between Cheri and me trivial—miniscule. So, I cranked up the car and drove back to Queens.

❦

The first thing I did that day was call Cheri and say, "Let's talk." We got together, and, amazingly, Cheri admitted to being wrong about everything.

Just kidding. That part didn't happen. In fact, it no longer mattered who was right or wrong. What mattered was that we were both alive. We both had our health.

Cheri must have thought I was crazy because the issue that seemed so important to me the night before was no longer an issue. As I mentioned before, I can't even remember what the argument was all about.

An early morning drive to New Jersey put it all in perspective.

STUDY QUESTIONS

- Do you tend to have more anxiety during the day or at night? Do you know why?

- Whom could you contact at two o'clock in the morning if you desperately needed to talk with someone?

- What would you have done had you been in Billy's shoes and were unable to go to sleep after having an argument with a significant person in your life?

- The big car accident reframed Billy's argument with Cheri. Have you ever had an experience that put a troubling situation in perspective for you? What happened?

- Why does it often take a dramatic event to help put things in perspective?

- What can you do to help put things in perspective without having to experience a dramatic event?

- What will you remember most from this story?

THE YAPPING DOG

My son Wendell was a musical theatre major at Valdosta State University. During the summer, Valdosta State has a program in which professional actors come in to perform in several shows with some of the college students. In 2015, Wendell was part of this summer-stock experience. He was in two shows, *Les Miserables* and *The Little Mermaid*.

A slew of us from Savannah planned to travel down to see him in *Les Miserables*. We would need to spend the night in Valdosta. My wife, Cheri, is an expert at getting good rates at hotels. Before we went to Valdosta, she said, "I found a good one! It's a 9-Star Hotel! Not only do they give you breakfast, but they also give you supper! They even have popcorn waiting for you in the lobby when you arrive. We can get it all for around $39." Maybe it was a little bit more, but it *was* a bargain.

I said, "That sounds good—a 9-star hotel, breakfast, supper, popcorn, $39 or a little bit more. What's the catch?"

She said, "Well, they do allow dogs."

I said, "Oh."

That was not good news to me, and Cheri knew it. Once, Cheri got us a deal at a dog hotel, and I spent the whole time dodging "mine fields." Not only did they have an issue outside the hotel in the parking lot, but they also had issues inside the hotel. I had said, "Never again!"

Don't get me wrong. I love dogs. I've always had a dog—at times, a slew of them. But I did not want to be vacationing at a hotel and constantly be playing hopscotch and holding my nose. That was not my idea of fun and relaxation.

She said, "But it's a 9-star hotel with free breakfast, free supper, popcorn."

She and I went back and forth about the dog issue. She finally talked me into trying the hotel, but not before I said that we would be regretting it.

Many family members and friends caravanned to South Georgia to see Wendell in the show and to stay in the wonderful dog hotel. When we arrived, I was surprised. The hotel looked immaculate, spotless. Everything was shining! And it didn't smell of canines. No one would ever guess that it was a dog hotel.

I thought, "This is too good to be true. Just you wait, Cheri Hester—just you wait. There are going to be some dog issues before we leave."

All of the Savannahians went to their rooms, which were just as nice and clean as the lobby. Since we had a large group with us, Cheri and I chose to get a suite. It had a front room with a pull-out sofa and a bedroom with two large beds. Cheri and I would take one bed. Our Minister of Music, Ray Ellis, who joined us on the trip, took the other.

Wendell, his brother Wesley, and their friend Colin

would use the pull-out sofa. I know that sounds cramped for three college age boys to be sharing a sofa bed, but the three of them had been sleeping together since they were five years old. They could handle it for one night.

Right across the hall, we got another room with two big beds for my daughter Christi, my mother Joan, and my cousin Kim. All for $39 or a little bit more.

It was time to go downstairs to eat the *free* supper before we went to the show. I was ready before everyone else, so I went there by myself. As I was walking down our hall to the elevator, I heard it: *Ruff, ruff, ruff. Ruff. Ruff. Ruff.*

There was a dog in the room right across the hall from us! It was in the room right next to my mother's room. By the sound of its bark, it was a good-sized dog. I was thinking, "If they are going to allow dogs in this place, why don't they at least put them all on the same floor? Why are they putting them on the floor with people who don't have dogs? I mean, Marmaduke is in the room right next door!"

I went downstairs for supper, thinking that the dog hotel would have only hotdogs and Kibbles 'n Bits for food options. To my surprise, they had a decent choice of foods. Along with hotdogs, they had chicken strips, baked potatoes, macaroni and cheese—about every carbohydrate and starch anyone could imagine. They also had soup and salad, which pleased Cheri.

We all ate, went to the theatre, and saw a wonderful production of *Les Miserables*. Wendell did a terrific job. He played one of the revolutionary students. At the climax of the show, the students had a big battle against the French soldiers and all the students got killed. Fighting valiantly to the bitter end, Wendell was the very last student to die. He died well.

After the show, we took Wendell out to eat. We got to the restaurant very late because *Les Miserables* is a long show. By the time we ate and got back to the hotel, it was 1:30 in the morning. We were exhausted. We had made the long drive to Valdosta. We saw a long show. We stayed up late. We were ready for a good night's sleep.

Wendell had to get up early because he had a rehearsal for the other show, *The Little Mermaid*. The theatre company was rehearsing *The Little Mermaid* during the day and performing *Les Miserables* at night. Everyone was exhausted and ready to go to bed.

Ray, Cheri, and I were in the bedroom. The three boys were on the sofa-bed in the front-room. The three ladies were in the room across the hall, with Marmaduke on one side of them and, probably, Rin Tin Tin on the other.

At 4:30 in the morning—4:30 in the morning—I started hearing: *Ruff, ruff, ruff. Ruff. Ruff. Ruff.* It just kept going on and on!

I had slept only three hours. Cheri, who was beside me, had not said a thing. She hadn't moved. But I knew she had to be awake. She is a light sleeper—a lot lighter than I am. If the dog woke me up, I'm sure it woke her up. But she was not saying anything. She obviously was pretending that this wasn't happening.

Now I didn't dare say something to her. If I did, she'd get mad and tell me that I woke her up. To make sure she was hearing what I was hearing and to make sure she knew that I knew what I was hearing, I decided to do some restless turning in the bed. And, every time I turned in the bed, I groaned.

Finally, after ten minutes of me tossing, turning, and groaning, the dog stopped barking.

But then, ten minutes later, it started again: *Ruff, ruff, ruff. Ruff. Ruff. Ruff.* This time, it didn't stop. It just kept yapping and yapping and yapping. I kept turning, groaning, and grunting, making sure that Cheri was aware of my displeasure.

Ray, who was in the other bed, spoke up. "This is unbelievable," he said. "This hotel needs to give everyone on this floor their money back."

Cheri finally chirped in, "Yes, this is pretty bad."

By now I was very frustrated. The owners can't be in their room. They must have gone downstairs to eat breakfast, or maybe they went out to the Cracker Barrel and left their dog in the room to wake everyone else up. What a selfish thing to do!

After twenty minutes of constant barking, I got out of bed. I had to see what room this yapping was coming from. It was still very dark, so I started slowly creeping to the door, trying to make sure I didn't wake up the three boys in the front room. I had no idea how they were sleeping through the barking dog, but they still seemed to be knocked out.

After I tiptoed by the boys, I reached for the knob of the front door. As I did, I noticed that the barking sound was very, very close. It sounded like it was in the hall! Had the dog gotten out of its room? Was the dog right outside our door?

Then I realized that the barking sounded even closer. It sounded as though the dog was inside our room! I couldn't believe it. Had the boys found a stray and not told us?

In the dark, I tried to follow the sound so I could locate the dog. It led me over to where the boys were sleeping. Then I saw it. The dog was right beside my sleeping son, Wendell. It looked very much like a cell phone. My son had turned his cell phone into an alarm clock. Guess what sound he was using for the alarm?

A yapping dog!

I said, "Wendell! Wendell! Turn that thing off! Turn it off! We'll get you up when it's time for you to get up." We later learned that Wendell had a ritual of starting his alarm clock two hours before he needed to get up, so that by the twentieth time it rang (or barked), he was up.

I couldn't believe it. I shook my head in frustration. But the worst part was that I had to go back to the bed and admit to Cheri that I wasn't right after all.

While the apostle Paul was in a Roman prison waiting to be executed, he wrote an incredible letter to the church in Philippi. In the second chapter of Philippians, he offered a picture of what it means to love. He wrote, "Do nothing out of selfish ambition or vain conceit" (Philippians 1:3a). I understand that the Greek words in this text actually mean, "Don't compete with each other. Don't be so competitive. Take the competition out of the relationship."

One reason this is so difficult for many of us to do is because there's an element of competitiveness in our DNA. It's part of our survival mode. If you were trying to survive in a primitive and hostile world, you needed to be competitive. There's something in us that prompts us to compete. This competitive nature may help us survive in a hostile world, but it's deadening for relationships.

To make it even more challenging, we live in a world that breeds competition. We've been encouraged and taught to compete as soon as we learn to walk and talk. It involves almost everything we do—from scholastics to athletics and everything in between. It's hard to turn it off. It's no wonder that we have so many problems with our family and friends.

Paul wrote, "Do nothing out of vain conceit." He was saying, "Get rid of an I-need-to-be-better-than-you attitude—take all of that out." Then he says, "Rather, in humility, value others above yourself" (Philippians 1:3b). Some translations read: "Consider others more important than yourself."

In 2015, I officiated a funeral in Plains, Georgia, for one of my church members named Tim Rockwell. Tim's parents had been close friends with President Jimmy Carter, so we were blessed to have President Carter participate in the service. He's a man I greatly admire, not only because he was president, but also because of the kind of life he has lived. If President Carter had told me to go jump in a lake, I probably would've jumped in a lake. Because when we're around someone more important than we are, we always defer to them. We laugh at their jokes. We don't correct their stories. We wish them well.

I know that in God's eyes no one is more important than anyone else. We are all loved and valued by our Creator. But that's not the point. What Paul is saying is to *act* as if they are more important than you.

I'm afraid that Cheri is stuck with a guy who always wants to be right—even about dog hotels. But I hope she's also stuck with a guy who is learning that it's okay not to be right, a guy who is trying to treat others as though they are more important than he is.

By the way, dogs are really good at doing that. As Josh Billings, the 19th century humorist, said, "A dog is the only thing on earth that loves you more than he loves himself." Maybe I need to stay at dog hotels more often. Maybe some of their goodness will rub off on me.

STUDY QUESTIONS

- Do you have any good dog-hotel stories?

- Do you consider yourself to be a competitive person? What things are you usually competitive about?

- What's the difference between wanting to win, trying to win, and needing to win?

- How do you think competitive feelings influence our society (within families, within communities, within country, and globally)?

- Can you think of a situation where pride was evident in your life recently? What is an effective antidote for your pride?

- What do you think about the phrase made popular by Dr. Phil, "Would you rather be right, or would you rather be happy?"

- What will you remember most from this story?

WATCHING M*A*S*H WITH THE FLU

I n January of 2015, I got a really bad case of the flu. To deal with the aches, pains, and high fever, I feasted on Theraflu. My other strategy for dealing with the pain was watching television. Flicking through channels, I came upon an episode of M*A*S*H.

M*A*S*H, of course, was a popular show from 1972 to 1983. The setting was an army surgical hospital in South Korea during the Korean War. The show was filled with memorable characters like Hawkeye, Radar, Hot Lips Houlihan, and Klinger. Its final show was the most-watched episode in television history at the time. It had a huge fan base.

I didn't watch a lot of the original episodes of M*A*S*H when it aired on television. For many years, it came on Monday nights at 9:00, and I would have been watching Monday Night Football. But there were some special episodes of M*A*S*H that I watched. I remember one about a bombardier who got shot down. He was unconscious, taken to the MASH (Mobile Army Surgical Hospital) unit, where he wakes up believing he is Jesus. He really thinks he is Jesus.

Before the end of the show, you start wondering yourself. If you ever get a chance, watch that episode. It's a good one.

Anyway, I was in bed with high fever, flicking the channels to see what might be on television. Normally, I would not have stopped when I landed on the channel *M*A*S*H* was on, but I had to stop because Radar was looking right at me and talking to me—I mean the character Radar was actually talking to me. I was in bed, and Radar came close to the screen and stared down at me on the bed. He asked me something, and he was waiting for me to respond. I looked over at my medication to see how much I had taken. Was I hallucinating?

Radar was looking down at me on my bed and he said, "How are you doing? Are you in much pain?"

I said, "Yes, Radar. Help me!"

Then he started to try to pick me up—he actually tried to lift me up. And he said, "My, you're a heavy one. I think I'm going to need some help lifting you." That comment made me feel even worse!

Then I realized what was happening. The camera was filming from a stretcher—from the perspective of a wounded soldier on a stretcher. The camera acted as the eyes of the soldier for the entire episode. You never saw what the wounded soldier looked like because you (the viewer) were his eyes. He had injured his throat and neck in battle, and he could no longer talk. So, the entire episode was from the perspective of a wounded soldier on a bed, and he couldn't talk. All he could do was observe and listen.

The man in charge of the MASH unit was Colonel Potter. Potter was a very pleasant, easy-going, older man who knew how to stay calm in chaotic situations. But in this particular episode, Colonel Potter was angry about something. He was on edge, snapping at everyone; nobody knew why.

A couple of days passed by, and Colonel Potter came to the bedside of the silent soldier. He said, "Hello, Private. I'm Colonel Potter." The right hand of the soldier reached out to shake Potter's hand. Potter responded by shaking the hand. Then he said, "Where are you from?" By this time, the soldier was able to write things on a small, handheld chalkboard. He wrote the word "Texas." Potter said, "You know, every soldier from Texas that's ever come through this unit has always had a good handshake."

Potter continued, "I make it a point to meet every soldier that comes through this unit. I'm sorry that it's taken me a couple of days to come to meet you. It's just that my mind's been a little preoccupied. You see, I have a wife at home. She's the best thing that ever happened to me. I would do anything for Mildred. I miss her terribly. But would you believe I forgot our anniversary? I was just so preoccupied by things here, but how could I have forgotten?" He left the bedside.

A little later, Hawkeye came to check on the soldier. As Hawkeye was talking to him, the soldier started writing on the chalkboard. He wrote, "Forgot his anniversary." And Hawkeye said, "OOOOH—so that's it." I could see that Hawkeye was starting to plan something that would remedy the situation.

Unfortunately, my meds kicked in at that point, and I dozed off with about fifteen minutes left in the show. I woke up right at the end, when they were waving goodbye to the soldier, who was well enough to be sent home. Everyone was happy, including Colonel Potter. I don't know what they did to make Colonel Potter happy, but I'm sure Hawkeye cooked up something wonderful. But the reason everything worked out was because someone listened. The wounded soldier couldn't talk, but he was listening intently.

Every other character in the show wanted to know what was wrong with Potter, but they were always so busy talking and doing things. They never could figure it out. It was the person who couldn't talk, who could only listen, who solved the problem.

The great Swiss psychiatrist, Dr. Paul Tournier was a spiritual giant. He believed that not listening was one of the world's major issues. He said, "Listen to all the conversations of our world, between nations as well as individuals. They are, for the most part, dialogues of the deaf."

Tournier said, "In order to really understand, we need to listen, not reply. We need to listen long and attentively. In order to help anybody to open his or her heart, we have to give them time, asking only a few questions, as carefully as possible, in order to help them better explain their experience."

Most of the time, in this fast-paced, noisy world, it is challenging to be a good listener. Sometimes, we are quiet if someone is talking to us, but we're not really listening to them. We're thinking about what we want to say, and we're just waiting for the other person to stop talking. Then, when they are quiet, we express our thoughts and opinions. What we keep doing is offering monologues to each other.

Listening is one of the most effective ways we can show

love. I'm not sure we can really love without listening. We can feel sentiment, and we can tell people how much we care about them, but until we get to the point where we can center in on the other and listen, we don't love effectively.

What would happen if we pretended to be the wounded soldier in M*A*S*H? What would happen if we spent most of our time listening instead of talking? Perhaps we could create a world where we would need no more wars and no more MASH units.

STUDY QUESTIONS

- What is your favorite *M*A*S*H* episode?

- Why do you think Colonel Potter poured his heart out to the wounded soldier, who was a stranger, instead of to his coworkers?

- Do you consider yourself to be a good listener?

- What makes many of us try to be early solutionists instead of patient listeners?

- Do you ask yourself, "What can I learn from what I'm hearing?"

- How has technology (cell phones, computers, television, etc.) impacted listening to others?

- When was the last time your tongue, texting, or tweeting got you in trouble? What have you found helpful in controlling your tongue?

- It has been said that the better we are at listening to people, the better we are at listening to God. Do you agree or disagree? Why?

- What will you remember most from this story?

WORDS TO A MOTHER

One of the most challenging illnesses for families to deal with is dementia. It seems to pounce on the brightest of people, as was the case with my father-in-law and mother-in-law. Cheri and I have experienced the difficult journey of having loved ones suffer a slow but steady decline of mental and physical health. I also have experienced it among my parishioners and their families.

❦

The Fritts sisters were twins who grew up at Asbury Memorial. By the time I met Jean and Jewel Fritts in 1993, both of them had married, raised children, traveled the world, and were sixty-six years old. Jean Fritts had become Jean Stewart and Jewel Fritts was now Jewel Nieuwstraten. The sixty-six-year-old sisters were the youngest members of Asbury Memorial when I first started my ministry at the church.

Jean was a tremendous help to me. In her younger days, she had served as the church secretary, so she was a great resource and a wealth of information. She helped me navigate my way through the committees and personalities of the church during my first years at Asbury Memorial. She served on various committees of the church and served as our church historian.

Jewel's health prevented her from being as active at the church. But she had led an active life, raising four adventurous children.

When Jewel made her transition on October 19, 2016, I met with her children to plan the funeral service. Jan, George, Julie, and Jill told me that their mother helped them have a wonderful childhood. They said they had been rambunctious children, loving the outdoors and loving animals. Many of the critters that made it to the "Nieuwstraten Hotel" were cats, dogs, turtles, fish, lizards, gerbils, hamsters, chickens, raccoons, 'possums, armadillos, owls, sparrows, geckos, salamanders, rabbits, guinea pigs, and snakes. Young George was especially adept at finding snakes. If they didn't stay at the house, he would take them to the nearby Science Museum so the viewing public could experience them.

Horses are not on this list, but they certainly were part of their lives too. Julie and Jill loved horses. Since they had no place to keep them, Jewel arranged for her daughters to take care of a friend's eighteen horses. For years, Jewel would drive Julie and Jill to the stables so they could care for the horses. In return, they were able to ride them.

Since the Nieuwstraten's house was half zoo, one might be surprised to learn that the matriarch was a "lady of ladies." But Jewel knew that her kids needed to be kids. She knew it was healthy for them to love nature and to be outdoors. She knew that a little dirt and some animals came with the territory.

One of her children said, "Growing up on a dirt street, with mostly boys in the neighborhood, mom had her hands full with an incredibly busy boy and three rough-and-tumble girls. Mom's neighbors would often praise her for keeping us clean, saying, 'Your mom must bathe you kids three times a day.' Mom was such a lady that she refused to holler our names through the neighborhood when she needed us home. She wouldn't yell out our names like the other parents did for their kids. She would simply walk out to the end of the driveway and begin to clap loudly. Eventually, everyone in the neighborhood learned to let us know. 'Your mom is clapping for you. Time to go.'"

❦

Jewel and her husband, George, met when friends introduced them while on Tybee Island, the beach close to Savannah. They married on New Year's Eve in 1953. After forty-seven years of marriage, George died in 2000.

After George's death, Jewel moved in with her daughter Julie and Julie's husband, James. It was during this time that Jewel's memory started slipping. As it always does, the disease eventually got hold of Jewel, stripping away layers of memories. Julie and James did a wonderful job of caring for Jewel until her death.

During the funeral service, I shared a special memory that daughter Jill had of her mother during her illness. One day, Jill walked into her mother's room and found Jewel looking sad. Jewel was trying her best to hold back tears. She did not want Jill to know that she had been upset and crying

Jill wrote:

Dementia had transitioned my mother's mind to a time

160

when she was, I'm guessing, in her early twenties. I could tell Mom recognized my face, but she seemingly didn't place me as her child. I assumed she just knew I was a familiar face. She began to tell me how she just found out that her boyfriend, whom she thought she was going to marry, had run off and married another girl. It was all so real to her. She was very sad and hurt, and it was difficult to see my mother cry. It was the most incredible experience for me to comfort her that day. I sat on the bed next to my mother. I wiped her tears and put a tissue in one hand as I picked up her other hand and placed it in mine. I told my mother that I was so sorry for the pain that she was going through. I told her that I wished I could take that pain away.

I then said, "I can't even begin to tell you how I know this, but there is one thing I can tell you right now. With God as my witness, I promise you, there is a man, a very handsome, funny, and kind man, who is going to come into your life and sweep you right off your feet. He is going to make you forget about this silly man you are upset about because he is going to truly love you forever. You and this wonderful man will be in love and have a beautiful family with daughters you can dress up like living dolls who will love you with all their heart and an amazing son who will love his mother like no one else in the world could. I promise you I know it — without a shadow of a doubt.

Mom looked at me with a glimmer of a smile and said, "You really think so?"

And I replied, "I promise you. I know so. I guarantee it."

I love what Jill said to her mother. It was brilliant. Two

thousand years ago, a man came to people and said, "I can't even begin to tell you how I know this, but there is one thing I can tell you right now. With God as my witness, I promise you that everything is going to be okay. In my father's house are many rooms. I have prepared a wonderful place for you. And there, you will truly be loved forever. You will forget about all the pain and suffering you have been through. You will experience true joy and incredible peace. I promise you. I know it—without a shadow of a doubt."

His friends looked at him and said, "You really think so?"

He replied, "I promise you. I know so. I guarantee it."

STUDY QUESTIONS

- Do you have family members or close friends with dementia? If so, what has been the most challenging part of the illness?

- What resources do you have to help provide long-term care for them?

- If you found yourself in a situation where you didn't know what to do or what to say or how to give the right care to meet a loved one's needs, what would you do?

- In dementia care, roles change and new challenges crop up, sometimes requiring us to do things we don't even think about and have never done before. Has that happened to you? How were you able to solve it?

- What do you think it would be like to forget the names and faces of the family members around you?

- Jill used a very creative and sensitive approach to comfort her mother. Have you found special ways or things to do to comfort your loved ones with dementia?

- What will you remember most from this story?

Mixing Religion and Politics

On a sunny Saturday afternoon in 1968, when I was nine years old, I was mowing the lawn at my house on the corner of 65th Street and Abercorn. A cool-looking, old-fashioned, Ford Model T came down the street and parked in front of my house. It had colorful flags, banners, and posters on it. A tall man with a big smile stepped out of the car and came over to me. I turned off the mower.

"Are you Wendell Hester's son?" he said.

"Yes, sir," I said.

"I knew your dad. In fact, we're related. We're cousins." I had never seen the man before in my life. But that didn't mean anything. My Grandmother Hester had nineteen siblings and my Grandfather Hester had nine, so there were relatives all over the place I didn't know.

The man continued, "I wonder if you could help me out. I'm the campaign manager for Jim Smith (that wasn't the politician's real name—I don't remember his name or what he was running for)." My newly-discovered relative continued, "I will give you a whole dollar if you go around and pass out all of these flyers for me." He had a big stack of paper flyers that promoted the person running for office.

A dollar for a nine-year-old boy in 1968 was a fair piece of change—a buck could get me four packs of baseball cards. He handed me the flyers and started to give me a dollar bill. Before he let go of it, he said, "Now, promise me that you'll pass every single one of these out. Okay?"

"I promise," I said. He hopped back into the fancy car and took off. I finished mowing the lawn and started on my journey to distribute the flyers. I went door to door, putting them in mailboxes, on doormats, on doorknockers—anywhere I felt people would find them. I went two blocks east, two blocks north, two blocks west, and two blocks south of my house.

I don't remember if it was because it had gotten dark or because I had gone as far from home as a nine-year-old boy should go by himself, but I stopped. I still had about sixty-five flyers left. I had run out of time and run out of houses. What was I to do? I had promised the man that I would pass out every single flyer.

Then a brilliant idea came to me! I had the perfect solution!

The next morning, my mother, sister, and I got up early to go to Sunday School. When we arrived at church, I didn't go directly to my class. I made a detour to the sanctuary. No one was there because everyone was in their Sunday School classes. So, I went row by row, pew by pew, and placed a campaign flyer at every spot where someone would be sitting. I also put them in the racks that held the visitor welcome cards and the offering envelopes. I even went up to where the preacher preached and put one on the pulpit. Can you imagine the look on that minister's face when he got up to preach and saw the flyer on his Bible?

At that age, I didn't realize that I had done something wrong. I was trying not to break my promise. But looking back, I can't believe I did what I did. Amazingly, I did not get lectured or punished — probably because I don't think anyone ever found out who did it. But you can be sure that it was the main topic of conversation at the next Administrative Board meeting.

❧

Please, do not do what I did, which is against the law. Churches and nonprofits are not supposed to engage in political campaigning for individuals running for office. However, we *can* and *should* talk about political issues. We should talk about what's right and what's wrong.

One of the great prophetic voices in the 20th century was William Sloan Coffin, former pastor at Riverside Church in New York. One Palm Sunday Service, he said, "Don't believe that Jesus was only a spiritual messiah and not a political one. That's the great Palm Sunday cop-out that will be proclaimed from pulpits all over the land today. Had Jesus been as apolitical as these pulpiteers, you can be sure the nails never would have grazed his hands."

Sometimes people get the phrase "Don't mix religion and politics" confused with the concept of the separation of church and state. The separation of church and state is intended to protect religious freedom. It supports our religious liberty and diversity.

That's very different from mixing religion and politics.

Mixing Religion and Politics

Religion shapes our moral conscience—or at least it should, and *politics* helps us *live out* that conscience. My religion helps me to determine what I believe is right and wrong, and politics gives me the tool to express those beliefs—be it by whom or what I vote for, whom or what issues I support, or whom or what I march for or protest against.

My hunch is that most of the people who say, "Don't mix religion and politics," usually are people who have it pretty good in life. They're pretty content with the status quo.

The problem is not that we shouldn't mix religion and politics. The problem is that we don't do it enough. The problem is that we don't take it seriously enough—that we don't do our homework on policies and politicians. But if a person wants to take their religion seriously, he or she needs to take their politics seriously. They go hand in hand.

This is God's world. Those who love God and God's creation should do all we can to take care of God's world. The systemic way we're supposed to do that is through politics—city, state, national, and global. Of course, there are other ways we can help the world, and we should do that. But the only way we can change the world systemically is through politics. It is my belief that this is what Jesus was trying to do when he left the countryside of Galilee to go to the big city of Jerusalem.

Theologian and historian Marcus Borg reminded us that crucifixion was a *political* form of execution. It wasn't used for ordinary criminals, not even for ordinary murderers. It was used specifically for political foes—for those who had chosen the path of resistance against established authority.

And when we say it was a political execution, we don't

mean simply that the *cause* was political, but that the *means* was political. Crucifixion, with all its brutality and its publicness, was meant to be a deterrent against standing against the powers that be. It says, "This is what happens to those who defy the authority of empire. We strip you. We beat you. Then we hang you up on a cross, so everyone can see you in all of your humiliation—so that everybody can see what happens to anyone who goes against the authorities."

In describing Jesus, Madeleine L'Engle recalled a line from T. S. Elliot: "Do I dare disturb the universe?" L'Engle said that Jesus was a "Universe-Disturber"—that it got him crucified and that to follow his way is to be a universe-disturber.

Like it or not, Jesus mixed religion and politics. And he showed us the way to do it.

Mahatma Gandhi must have been reflecting on the life of Christ when he said:

"To refuse to struggle against the evil of the world is to surrender your humanity.

To struggle against the evil of the world with the weapons of the evil-doer is to enter your humanity.

To struggle against the evil of the world with the weapons of God is to enter your divinity."

The Jewish philosopher Abraham Joshua Heschel once said that "religion begins in mysticism but ends in politics." Maybe that's why I didn't get into trouble when I was nine years old. Maybe the minister realized that, although I went about it the wrong way, I was not far off from understanding what the Gospel message is all about.

STUDY QUESTIONS

- Were you brought up hearing, "Don't mix religion and politics"? What was said at your house about religion and politics?

- Why do you think we often hear people say, "Don't mix religion and politics"? What are the concerns?

- What are your thoughts on the statement, "Religion shapes our moral conscience, and politics helps us to live out that conscience"?

- What are your thoughts on the statement, "Jesus was a Universe-Disturber, and it got him crucified. To follow his way is to be a universe-disturber"?

- What's the purpose of the church if it doesn't the address the concerns of society?

- What are some social and/or political issues that are appropriate for the church to address?

- What issues do you feel that the church does not speak out about enough?

- What will you remember most from this story?

WHAT I LEARNED AT THE MASTERS

My Uncle Phil picked me up at 6:00 a.m. on April 10, 2002, to take me to my first Masters Golf Tournament in Augusta, Georgia. Actually, we were going the day before the Tournament began for what is called "Fun Day" or "Fan Day." This is the day the golfers are practicing. The atmosphere is more relaxed. People bring cameras and take pictures of the glorious golf course and their favorite golfers.

As we made the two-hour-and-forty-minute drive up Highway 21 to Augusta, we were concerned that the event might get rained out. The sky was overcast, and we kept driving in and out of rain. But like the other thousands of fans, we would brave the day with umbrellas to experience this special event. I am not the world's biggest golf fan, but if you get a chance to go to the Super Bowl or to the World Series, you go!

When we arrived, it was raining, so my uncle and I squeezed under one big umbrella and dodged other people as we fumbled for our tickets, making sure the security guards and ticket-takers knew that we *belonged*. Not long after we walked through the gates, the rain stopped, and we approached the beautiful golf course with its blooming azaleas.

We saw the famous Amen Corner. We saw the Eisenhower Tree that always enticed Ike's ball. We watched the players practice on the driving range and putting green. We walked all over the course to various holes. We wondered if we would see the mighty Tiger. We saw him right away. In fact, everywhere we went we saw Tiger. It was like he was following us.

We decided to take a break for lunch and have some of the famous pimento cheese sandwiches. Augusta is a special place—if I sold those sandwiches on a corner in Savannah, I'd make about $8. They, however, sold about eight million dollars' worth that day. Augusta is indeed unique.

It was now the afternoon, and we had walked to the other end of the golf course. It just so happened that a family member of one of our church members had died the night before. I was feeling guilty about being at The Masters during this family's time of grief. I had brought my cell phone, so I could at least call them and let them know that I was thinking about them.

Even though this was Fun Day at The Masters and people had their cameras out taking pictures, I knew I should not make a phone call anywhere near the golfers. That's not good golf etiquette. So, I walked away from the golfers and went near a clubhouse restroom area. I took out my phone, turned it on, and dialed the number. Just as the grieving family answered the phone, a man rushed up to me and said, "Buddy, you better put that away. They'll take it away from you."

I said, "Really? I didn't know. Thanks for letting me know." The guy said it in such an alarming way that I turned the phone off in the middle of the conversation.

After I put the phone back in my pocket, I looked up. About twenty-five yards away, I saw a guy, another golf fan, talking to a security guard. While he was talking, the golf fan was pointing in my direction. I was thinking, "Surely he's not telling the security guard about me, is he? No, you're just imagining things. You're being paranoid." But then the security guard started walking in my direction.

I started to walk the other way, but then I said to myself, "This is ridiculous. If he needs to talk to me, he needs to talk to me." The security guard, who could have been Barney Fife's twin, came up to me and said, "Do you have a cell phone?" The attitude and tone of his voice reminded me of how Barney sounded after he caught someone jaywalking.

I said, "Yes, I do."

He said, "That's against the rules."

I said, "I'm sorry. Someone just told me that. I didn't realize it."

"Give me your cell phone."

As I gave him my phone, Barney turned on his hand-held radio and said, "Charlie, I've got a *Thirty-Two* over here— send someone over."

"Hey, I'm really sorry," I said. "I'm a minister. There happened to be a death of someone in my congregation, and I needed to check on the family." No response. "I wasn't by the players. I didn't even have the power on until I made the call." Again, no response.

Instead, my uncle and I were whisked over to another security guard and then to a make-shift tent where they hold criminals at The Masters. Several people there told us that we would have to leave—that we were being kicked out and that someone would escort us out. Apparently, there had been a sign at the entrance that read "No Cell Phones." I tried to explain that it had been raining and that, with all the umbrellas and people, I had not seen the sign. I explained again that I was a minister, there had been a death, and I was calling a grieving family. It did not matter.

Rarely do I tell people that I'm a minister, and rarely do I wear my religion on my sleeve; but it seemed to me that these folks needed a little religion. So, I commenced telling them about the *letter* of the law and the *spirit* of the law.

"Pastor," they said, "the folks around here just believe in the law."

It was then that I started hearing dueling banjos playing in the distance. "Is this really happening?" I wondered, "Are these people for real? We're really being kicked out?

I felt like I was in Mayberry talking to several Barney Fifes, with their bullets in their pockets proudly bragging about making an arrest. I just knew Andy would eventually show up and help the Barneys put things in perspective: "Now fellas, the pastor didn't see the sign. He was calling someone who had lost a loved one. We'll just hold his cell phone for him; and then, at the end of the day, he can come by and pick it up. That's the fair thing to do. Come on by, Pastor, on your way out and pick up your phone. Enjoy the rest of your visit!"

That's what I was waiting for. But Andy never showed

up.

So, we got escorted out, ridden out in a golf cart, by a very compassionate older man who drove the cart. He kept apologizing during the ride. We told him not to worry about it, that it wasn't his fault. In fact, it was actually pretty cool to be riding at The Masters because golf carts aren't allowed at Augusta National. Everyone—even golfers—even the great Tiger Woods—must walk. So, my uncle and I got a nice, private golf cart ride on the beautiful golf course.

We had been there a good while. We had seen a lot. Our feet were hurting, and we got a ride back to our car. We got to see the course from the privileged perspective of a golf cart. Everybody started looking at us like we were special.

And then, all of a sudden, the golf cart stopped. Apparently, some golfers were in the process of shooting in front of us. And, lo and behold, guess who it was! Tiger! I couldn't believe it. There he was again! I said, "Tiger, we're getting to ride in a golf cart at The Masters!" I waved at him— hoping he wouldn't notice the handcuffs. But I guess he did because he shouted back, "But I bet I'll be here a lot more times than you."

And he was right. But that was somewhat of a miracle when you think about it because for many years African-Americans were not allowed to be members at Augusta National. Do you know the year African-Americans were allowed to become members?

1970? Nope.

1980? Nope.

Try 1990.

It was not that African-Americans couldn't be at Augusta

National. They could be there. They just had to carry people's golf clubs. In fact, until 1983, the caddies at Augusta *had* to be African-American. "As long as I'm alive," said Clifford Roberts, one of the club's founders in 1933 and a longtime Masters chairman, "all golfers will be white, and all caddies will be black."

When I remembered this history—and remembered that women were not welcome until 2012—I felt kind of honored about being thrown out. I should not have been surprised that at Augusta National there was no Andy Taylor—there was no voice of reason, no calming presence.

Actually, there was one Andy Taylor there. He came in the person of my uncle. The whole situation had gotten me angry. I wasn't only angry at the Barneys, I was angry at myself and the situation. For the irony is that I don't like cell phones. I try to stay away from them as much as possible. But since I was going out of town, since we had a death at the church, and since there might be an emergency, I took it.

Worst of all, I felt horrible for my Uncle Phil. He had tried to do something nice for his nephew by taking me to The Masters, and I had done something that put him in a very embarrassing situation. But Uncle Phil handled it like a charm. I was the one acting more like Barney, and he had the calming spirit of Andy.

❧

My trip to The Masters reminded me that it is not so much the destination that counts, but the journey itself. As good as it was to get to see Tiger Woods, as good as it was to see the amazing landscape of the Augusta Golf Course, the best part of the trip was being with Uncle Phil—riding on Highway 21, telling jokes and stories, going through small towns like Sardis and Sylvania, learning about ancestors who had lived there, stopping for a country breakfast along the way. The Masters was just icing on the cake.

Yes, I wish the people at Augusta National would invest as much in their people skills as they do their putting greens. I wish they would treat people as well as they treat their fairways. But being thrown out of The Masters was not a big deal. We had experienced something bigger, something better, something more important. We had invested in the journey, not the destination.

This helped us put The Masters experience in perspective. It gave us a fabulous story for my uncle and me to tell at parties, and it gave me plenty of sermon material for Sundays. For Augusta National is not the only place that can do better with hospitality and people skills; churches can too. We all need to process how we treat people, even when they mess up—perhaps especially when they mess up.

Oh, one last thing:

If you ever get to go to The Masters, and at the end of the day you get really tired and don't feel like walking all the way back to your car, don't worry. All you have to do is pull out your cell phone, and the good folks at Augusta will be glad to give you a ride to your car.

STUDY QUESTIONS

- What do you see as the difference between the letter of the law and the spirit of the law?

- What are the dangers of not following the letter of the law?

- What are the dangers of not following the spirit of the law?

- Who are your Andy Taylors (or Angie Taylors)? Who are the people that are your voices of reason, who help you keep balanced, who help you laugh and keep calm?

- Which is more important, the journey or the destination?

- What is meant by the phrase, "Life is a journey, not a destination?"

- What will you remember most from this story?

TAKING PICTURES IN A HELICOPTER

T hanks to my generous in-laws, Cheri and I were able to go to Hawaii for our honeymoon. But things got off to a rocky start. Even though our flight went well, my suitcase didn't make it over the ocean. Then, Cheri woke up after our first day with either sun poisoning or food poisoning or both. The two of us looked like quite the pair.

We thought our luck had changed when we won a free helicopter ride around the island of Kauai. Cheri was very excited about the ride because she loves to take pictures. Cheri takes pictures every ten seconds when she is on vacation. I, on the other hand, don't own a camera.

Just before we were to get on the helicopter, we learned that we could not sit together. Since another couple also had won a free ride, we needed to distribute everyone's weight evenly. I would need to sit up front with the pilot, while Cheri would need to sit in the back with the other couple. I had the better view, so Cheri wanted me to take the pictures on this once-in-a-lifetime opportunity. Then Cheri said, "There are only three pictures left on this roll. After you take three pictures, you are going to have to change the film."

Taking Pictures from a Helicopter

Anyone who knows me knows that this was not a good scenario. Changing film in a camera could be challenging for me on the ground. I couldn't imagine doing it high in the air in a helicopter. Trying to be a good husband for my new wife on our honeymoon, I told her that I would do my best. Cheri had about thirty seconds to show me how to change the film before we had to get in the chopper.

We got on the helicopter, which was extremely loud. We each received a headset to put on, so we wouldn't go deaf. We went up in the air. I successfully took three pictures. Hooray! Now it was time to change the film. I had the camera and the new role of film in my lap studying it, trying to recall what Cheri told me to do. I felt a tap on my back. I turned my head to look back. It was Cheri yelling over the sound of the chopper, "Take a picture! Take a picture!" She was pointing at things that she wanted photographed.

I opened the camera, took out the used roll of film, and put the new roll in. I was to wrap one end of it around something and close the lid, which I tried to do. I was then supposed to push a button. But which button was it?

Apparently not the one I pushed because, when I pushed it, I heard this strange sound. It almost sounded like film being sucked up. And that's exactly what it was. When I pressed the button, the film went the wrong way. It literally got sucked up. I couldn't believe it. There was no more film for our once-in-a-lifetime helicopter ride in Hawaii.

Then there was more tapping on my back. "Come on! Take a picture of that! Take a picture of that!"

I looked down in my lap at the camera, trying to decide what to do. If I told Cheri what happened, there could be two possible results: She would be very sad and disappointed and probably wouldn't enjoy the rest of our once-in-a-lifetime experience. Or she would be so angry and frustrated that she would do something that would make us crash.

So, I did what any smart husband would do on his honeymoon. I *pretended* to take pictures! I wasn't about to have us all die in a fiery crash, and I didn't want to ruin this experience for Cheri. I started snapping away! I took all kinds of pictures. Left side, right side—all over the place!

When we landed and got in the car to leave, I said, "Cheri, before we go, there's something I need to tell you." I broke the news to her about the film and told her how sorry I was. "But I saw you taking pictures." she said. I explained why I did what I did, and, surprisingly, she took it amazingly well. Maybe it didn't totally surprise her. Perhaps she had known me long enough to anticipate some of my technological inadequacies. We decided that we would buy some post-cards and pretend that they were the pictures we made.

It was strange being in a situation where I purposely deceived my spouse. But looking back, I'm not sure I would have done things differently—other than putting the film in the camera correctly, of course. But I'm glad that I told Cheri about it as soon as we got in the car. I was tempted to keep the façade going, not say anything about it. When we got back to Georgia and developed the pictures, I could always blame it on the film.

But Cheri and I both believe that honesty is the best policy. During our courting years in the 1980s, we were big fans of educator John Bradshaw, who was known for saying,

"Families are as sick as their secrets." All too often, we had seen relationships between couples, families, and friends crumble because of secrets and dishonesty.

Many of those relationships could have been made whole through open and honest sharing, but, for some reason, those conversations never took place. My suspicion is that shame and embarrassment got in the way. They can get the best of any of us if we're not careful.

I guess the next time we get a chance to take pictures from a helicopter, I'll make sure that the film is changed on the ground before we take off. Either that, or I need to lose a lot of weight, so I can sit in the back and Cheri can sit up front with the pilot and take her pictures.

STUDY QUESTIONS

- Is it ever okay to be deceptive or not tell the truth?

- Someone once said, "There are lies, damned lies, and statistics." What do you think of this?

- Should Billy have told Cheri that he wasn't comfortable changing the film in the helicopter?

- Did Billy do the right thing by pretending to take pictures, or would you have done something differently?

- What role does trust play in your relationships with family and friends? How would these relationships be affected if you found out someone was lying to you?

- What do you think of the phrase, "We're as sick as our secrets"?

- What do pride and/or shame have to do with not being honest and open?

- What will you remember most from this story?

THE MOST POPULAR MAN IN NEW YORK CITY

When I was an actor in New York City in the 1980s, I was part of the Actors' Fellowship group at Marble Collegiate Church. Actors' Fellowship was a prayer and support group for people in the performing arts. We would gather on Monday evenings when most of the shows in New York City were dark.

I had been part of the group for a couple of years when a man named Del Willard started attending. Del was older than the rest of us in the group—most of the participants were in their twenties and thirties; Del was in his fifties or sixties. He was pursuing acting, but he made a living as a cab driver.

I had never met anyone like Del before. Most of the people I knew that were pursuing "the business" were younger. Most of the people I knew his age had families and had more-established jobs. And he was the only New York City cab driver I knew.

But the thing that made Del most unique was his manner of conversation. I had never heard anyone speak so openly about themselves, especially about their shortcomings. Del often calmly shared that he was a recovering alcoholic, that he had destroyed his marriage and the relationship he had with his family, that he had struggled with his temper, and that he wanted and needed more of God in his life.

Many of the people I knew who were Del's age and who attended church were much more private about their struggles. It's not that they were phony. It's just that they tended not to expose any of their problems or weaknesses.

Del Willard showed me a different model. It was one that he obviously learned from the twelve-step programs in which he was heavily involved. He was quite open about his dependence on God (or Higher Power). Long before I learned about the writings of Franciscan Richard Rohr, Del Willard told me about his struggles with the ego.

Del's courage and willingness to be vulnerable inspired the rest of us at Actors' Fellowship. His example encouraged us to speak not only from our minds, but also from our hearts. As a result, our studies and discussions created transforming moments and special friendships.

As much as I loved and admired Del, I felt sad for him. Because of his past actions, he had very little contact with any of his family members. He did not blame his family; he blamed himself. He said that he was the one who had been at fault. Due to his actions, they had every right to be upset with him. I could tell that he was saddened by their absence in his life.

Del, however, would become extremely joyful whenever he was in a situation in which he felt God's unconditional love. He had not felt this kind of love as a child from his father. The scars that came from emotional and physical abuse would shape Del into the person who turned to alcohol and violence. But his discovery of AA and the discovery of God's amazing grace transformed Del and his life.

After I went to seminary and started working at Marble Collegiate as a minister, Del and I would often get together for lunch. He would come by the church, and we would walk to a nearby diner. I loved these get-togethers because I always knew I was going to hear some honest sharing. We wouldn't be talking about the weather or the Yankees or the Knicks. We would be talking about life stuff—deep stuff, spiritual stuff. Del was always interested in stretching and growing. Don't get me wrong. I enjoyed lighter conversations too. But occasionally, it was nice to have some encounters of depth.

As much as I liked the conversations, my favorite part of the experience was walking with Del to the diner and walking from the diner back to the church. We often would pass homeless people camped out on the street. Instead of passing them by like I and everyone else did, Del would often go over to them, kneel down, and talk to them. It was as if he could communicate with them in a special way.

The other thing that would happen on our walks is that many people who passed by us would say, "Hello." At first, I thought they were nodding to me. I was the minister at a big Fifth Avenue church, and Del was a cab driver. But it soon became obvious that these were all Del's acquaintances. When we reached the diner, there would always be a customer there who knew Del too.

The way people greeted and nodded to Del was interesting. I could tell that these people admired him, looked up to him. It was if this common-looking, older guy in blue jeans and a plaid, button-down shirt was the Godfather or something.

I finally realized what was going on. These were people Del knew from AA. These were people he had spent time with and helped. By the number of people who greeted us, half of the people who lived and worked in Manhattan must have been in AA. The man who had no family seemed to be known and respected by every other person in Manhattan. The man who at one time was viewed as a drunkard and a failure ended up touching and helping multitudes of hurting people in one of the biggest cities in the world.

I once heard a minister say that Jesus came to teach us how to be human. I think Del Willard was one of his best students.

STUDY QUESTIONS

- Some have said that twelve-step programs are out-churching the church. What does that mean? Do you agree?

- How open are you about your dependence on God or Higher Power?

- What is the difference between honesty and full disclosure? Are they both always appropriate?

- Why do you think Del was able to lead a different life from the one that destroyed his marriage and family?

- How do you measure success? What is the meaning of having a successful life?

- Who are the people in your life that will talk with you about things other than sports or the weather or the latest movie—who will talk with you about the deeper things in life, spiritual things?

- What will you remember most from this story?

In Remembrance of Me

One of the great couples at Asbury Memorial was Frank and Grace St. George. Frank never missed a service or a church meeting, even when he got emphysema. He would always be there, even with an oxygen tank strapped to his back.

After Frank's death, Grace moved into a care facility with six other people. It was like a large, regular house, with a caretaker who oversaw seven elderly occupants.

One day I stopped by to see Grace and to bring her Holy Communion. The caretaker saw me go into Grace's room, and she asked me if it would be okay if all the residents had Communion. At first, I hesitated because I was concerned that there may be people of different faiths, and I didn't want to offend them. But then I realized that I could offer it and just make sure that everyone knew it was okay not to participate.

So, Grace and I went into the large common room where the other six residents had gathered. I asked each of them if they would like to participate in and be part of Communion. Each of them said, "Yes," except for one rather sullen-looking man.

He was husky and wore suspenders. He had a handsome face, even though it was twisted with an expression of anger and dissatisfaction. You could tell that he did not want to be bothered. He definitely did not want anything to do with me. That was fine; I wanted to respect where he was.

I then went into the kitchenette to prepare the elements of bread and juice that I would be serving. While I was pouring the juice into the tiny communion cups, the doorbell rang. The person at the door must have walked into the large room where everyone was sitting because the next thing I heard was a female voice saying, "Hey, Daddy!"

"Darling!" a man exclaimed, "What a nice surprise!" A conversation of love and affection continued between them.

When I returned to the big room with the Communion elements, I realized that the father of the woman who had just dropped by was the grumpy man who did not want Communion. I blessed the elements in front of everyone, and then I started passing them out saying, "Take; eat. Do this in remembrance of me."

You may have already guessed what happened next.

As I got near to where the old, husky, grumpy man was sitting, he extended his left hand with his palm up.

"Would you like Communion?" I asked.

"Yes, I would," he said.

As I gave him the elements and watched him partake, the old, twisted face was gone. It was now a face of joy and satisfaction.

After our little service was over, I packed up and started to leave, and the old man said to me, "Thank you. Come back again soon, would you?"

What happened? What happened to the man that day? It was as if I walked out of a room that had seven people in it; and when I came back, someone had left, and a new person had entered.

Maybe Communion happened. Maybe Communion always happens when someone is remembered.

STUDY QUESTIONS

- Have you ever experienced Holy Communion outside of a sanctuary or church building? What was the setting? What was the experience like?

- Have you ever taken Holy Communion to a homebound church member? What was the experience like?

- Why do you think the man changed his mind about receiving Holy Communion?

- What people have the greatest healing influence in your life?

- What does this story reveal about those who have felt forgotten?

- Do you visit people who are homebound or in nursing homes? If you do, what has the experience been like?

- What will you remember most from this story?

ONE MORE PRAYER

I had the privilege of officiating a private wedding ceremony for a groom named Bradley and a bride named Blaire. Earlier that day, Bradley had graduated from boot camp on Parris Island, South Carolina. There he stood in his uniform, looking younger than I ever remembered soldiers looking, holding the hands of his very beautiful bride.

I offered the introductory words of the ceremony and an opening prayer. Then came the exchange of vows and the exchange of rings. Both Bradley and Blaire were very present for each other during the ceremony. You could tell that they loved each other very much. I then put my hand on their hands and pronounced them husband and wife.

Whenever I officiate a wedding ceremony in a church, I usually offer a prayer at this point in the service, just before I say, "You may kiss the bride." But on this occasion, we were not in a church. I had just met Bradley and Blaire, and I didn't know how much their faith meant to them. When I looked at Bradley after pronouncing them husband and wife, he looked like he wanted to kiss Blaire so badly that I decided to skip the prayer. I went ahead and said, "You may kiss the bride."

And I was right. Bradley couldn't wait! During the ceremony he had been soldier-like, solemn, and unemotional as he said his vows. Blaire, on the other hand, wore her emotions on her sleeve. But when I pronounced them husband and wife, Bradley transformed right in front of our eyes. He broke into a huge grin that he couldn't contain as he gazed at Blaire. Anyone could tell that he couldn't wait to kiss his new wife. So, I went ahead and said, "You may now kiss the bride." And they gave each other a sincere, passionate, and fairly long kiss.

When they stopped kissing, something happened that has never happened in the thirty-one years I've officiated weddings. The groom looked at me and said, "Would you mind saying one more prayer for us?"

"Excuse me?" I thought.

I wish I could have seen the look on my face. After the kiss, the bride and groom have a party! After the kiss, the bride and groom walk down the aisle and hug each other. After the kiss, the bride and groom are greeted by well-wishers and focus on getting all those photographs.

But no! Bradley wanted one more prayer.

And Bradley was right. He and Blaire needed another prayer. Not only were they entering the challenges of marriage, but they also were embarking on a journey as a military family, which has its own unique fears and challenges.

So, I prayed the prayer that I usually offer at the end of wedding ceremonies:

We ask your blessings, O God, upon Bradley and Blaire.

Shower them with your grace, so that they may have strength and patience, affection and understanding, as they live and grow as individuals and as a couple. May they be to the other:

> *A strength in times of need,*
>
> *A comfort in times of sorrow,*
>
> *A counselor in times of perplexity,*
>
> *And a companion in times of joy.*

Then, before saying "Amen," I added words pertaining to this young couple's particular situation. It was a very meaningful and powerful moment.

We didn't know what was in store for Bradley's future. Would he be going into harm's way? Would he be coming back home safely? Even if he was not physically harmed, how would he be emotionally and mentally? And what about Blaire, the young bride living the challenging life of a military spouse? Prayer was indeed needed.

Good call, Bradley.

❦

I wish I was an expert on prayer. I really don't know anyone who is. Prayer is one of the most difficult aspects of faith. It can be mysterious, frustrating, fabulous, and confusing.

One of my favorite understandings of prayer occurs in *Shadowlands*, a play about British theologian and author C. S. Lewis and his relationship with an American divorcée named Joy Davidson Greshem.

In the play, Lewis has just returned home to Oxford from London. There, he and Joy were married in her room at the hospital where she was dying of cancer.

As Lewis arrives at the college where he teaches, he meets

Harry Harrington, an Episcopal priest. Harry asks him, "What news is there? How is everything?" C. S. Lewis hesitates, but decides to speak of the marriage and not of the cancer saying, "Good news, I think, Harry. Yes, good news."

Harry, not aware of the marriage and thinking that Lewis is referring to Joy's medical condition, says, "That's wonderful. I know how hard you've been praying. Now God is answering your prayer."

And C. S. Lewis says, "That's not why I pray, Harry. I pray because I can't help myself. I pray because I am helpless. I pray because the need flows out of me all the time, waking and sleeping. It doesn't change God. It changes me."

Every person has his or her own understanding and expectations of prayer. But it seems to me that its ultimate goal is the same for everyone: to put our future and our faith in God's loving embrace. I personally can do that better when I remember all the things for which I can be thankful and when I remember that I am totally dependent on God. If prayer helps us put our future and faith in God, then I think it's always a good idea to ask for one more prayer.

STUDY QUESTIONS

- Why do you think it was so important for Bradley to have one more prayer at the end of the wedding ceremony?

- What do you think C. S. Lewis meant when he said, "Prayer doesn't change God; it changes me"? Do you agree?

- How would you define prayer?

- With regard to your prayer life, what hinders you?

- With regard to your prayer life, what helps you?

- Billy describes one of the goals of prayer as putting our future and faith in God's loving embrace. What does that mean for you? How do you do it?

- What will you remember most from this story?

THE FASHION SHOW

R abbi Robert Haas is the rabbi for Congregation Mickve Israel in Savannah, Georgia. Mickve Israel is the third oldest Jewish congregation in the United States. Besides leading this wonderful congregation, Rabbi Haas does stand-up comedy. If you're ever in the Savannah area, check to see if the rabbi will be performing at a local club or event. He's fabulous!

Over the years, Rabbi Haas and I have become good friends. Not too long ago, he asked me if I would host a fundraiser to go toward finding a cure for Crohn's disease and colitis. The fundraiser was going to be at the Savannah Golf Club in the form of a fashion show. As the emcee, I was going to welcome everyone, introduce people, sing a song, and close the event. A piece of cake—I could do that.

The Fashion Show Fund Raiser was to be on a Thursday afternoon. On the Tuesday before the event I received a script through email. I looked over the script, saw where I was to welcome the audience, introduce speakers, and sing—like I said, "a piece of cake." But then at the bottom of the email was this sentence: "We'll send you the other script tomorrow."

What other script? What other script were they talking about?

The next night, the night before the event, I opened my email, and in the subject line were the words: "Fashion Show Script."

I opened it and realized that they also wanted me to emcee the actual fashion show. They wanted me to describe what the models were wearing—to describe the clothes.

This was not good news. The word "fashion" and my name NEVER have been used in the same sentence.

I looked at the script and the words were all Greek to me. I didn't know how to pronounce them. My wife, Cheri, didn't even know how to pronounce them. I spent the rest of the night on the Internet looking up words, trying to figure out what they meant and how to pronounce them. When I tried practicing them and reading the script out loud, Cheri would start howling. I was definitely a fish out of water.

I was hoping no one from my church would be at the event because I knew they would not be able to keep a straight face. Fortunately, Margaret Cook-Levy was the only church member there, and she did a great job of pretending that I didn't make a fool of myself.

Here are some of the things I had to say:

Amy is opening the show with our exquisite Cremieux Carter Velvet Jumpsuit in Evergreen. Velvet is a huge trend this holiday season.

For the adventurous ones, we have Jessica in this stylish yet comfortable IC Boho Harem style Jumpsuit. This piece is sure to be a show-stopper with its unique design and bold cobalt blue color.

Elaine is again showcasing a piece from the IC collection called the Boat Neck Asymmetrical Studded Tunic. This unique top is finished with a ZOZO Ankle Slim Leg Pant in the smoke color.

Shirley is displaying the Antonio Melani deep green Luxury Lesley Tie Cashmere Sweater. This design is unique due to the already sewn-in sleeves around the waist to give the illusion of another sweater tied, but one does not have the extra bulk of a second sweater. The luscious sweater is paired with Nygard Lux Black Plaid Leggings. Shirley finished her outfit with a spunky splash of color with this Gianni Bini Anna Multicolor Faux Fur Vest.

Oh, my goodness! I had to do seventeen of those! There were seventeen different outfits. Did I mention that the word "fashion" and my name NEVER have been used in the same sentence?

That is, until then!

Fortunately, everyone seemed to overlook my awkwardness; everyone seemed to have a good time. I realized that this was going to be a fun and nonjudgmental group when I saw that the door prize for the event was a jeweled toilet that could be used as a planter. That made me feel a lot better.

I usually only do things that I know I'm good at doing. It was scary for me to step out of my comfort zone. But things worked out really well. I met some wonderful people, had a great time, and hopefully helped raise a lot of money for a good cause.

❦

Margaret Cook-Levy told me that a few days later she was out shopping with a friend. They saw some nice clothes, and her friend said, "I recently heard somewhere that this style is really in right now."

Margaret chuckled to herself because she knew where her friend had heard it. She had heard it from Billy "Armani" Hester.

STUDY QUESTIONS

- What causes do you help support? Why do you support them?

- How do you like trying to do things that you are not good at doing?

- Why do many of us hesitate to do something we're not good at doing?

- What role did humor play in comforting Billy when he was out of his comfort zone?

- Have you done something out of your comfort zone lately? What was it? How did it go? How did it make you feel?

- How could you grow in this area of your life?

- What will you remember most from this story?

AN UNREALIZED PRESENCE

W hen my older daughter Chelsea was five-years-old and started attending school, it was very difficult for her three-year-old sister, Christi. Little Christi felt abandoned when Chelsea went off to school each day. She would miss her big sister terribly.

One night that year, our family was gathered in the girls' bedroom because Chelsea had lost her first tooth. We were all excited since the tooth fairy would be making her first visit to our house. My wife, Cheri, had recently read a book to the girls about the tooth fairy. This particular version conveyed that the tooth fairy would come while you were sleeping and not only would take your tooth, but also would take you. She'd take you for a ride among the stars because your tooth would become a star. Looking back, I'm not so sure that was a great story for young children. Sounds a bit scary to me.

Fortunately, the story didn't seem to bother Chelsea at all. She put her tooth under her pillow, hopped into bed, and excitedly said, "I'll be flying tonight!"

Christi, who slept in the same room with her big sister, was sprawled out on her bed, looking intently at Chelsea.

Then, with the saddest voice I had ever heard, she said "I'm going to miss you, Chelsea."

❧

Before I focus on Christi's lament, I want to say how surprised and impressed I was with Chelsea and her willingness to go on a trip with the tooth fairy. As a child and youth, I struggled with separation anxiety. Most of it stemmed from my father's death when I was four years old. I was concerned that something would happen to my mother too, so I didn't want to leave her. This got to be quite embarrassing whenever I had to go out of town with school or church groups.

I was one of the leaders on my football, baseball, and basketball teams, but, whenever we had road games, I would get on a bus, clam up, and tear up. I couldn't understand why the other players could be so relaxed and playful. Didn't they realize how fragile life was? Didn't they know this could be the last time we would see our parents and loved ones?

So how in the world could my five-year-old daughter be okay with the tooth fairy coming down and taking her for a ride among the stars? And how did that child grow up and have the courage to go off to do graduate studies in Colorado? And how did her little sister grow up, get in a car, and drive across the United States all by herself to live in California? Yes, the little girl who said, "I'm going to miss you, Chelsea," has ended up doing some flying of her own. The human spirit is amazing.

I'm so glad that my children don't seem to have the same separation anxiety that I struggled with for so long. But there are a lot of other things that cause people to have anxiety.

Most everyone struggles with something.

I still haven't mastered my anxieties and probably never will. But I have found something that has helped. It is the realization that we are never, ever alone. And that brings us back to Christi's lament: "I'm going to miss you, Chelsea."

Christi went to sleep thinking that her sister Chelsea would be leaving her that night. She believed there would be a time in the night when the tooth fairy would come and take Chelsea, leaving Christi all alone in her room. But unknown to Christi was the fact that Chelsea never left—she was right there with her the whole time. But she didn't know it because she was asleep.

Perhaps many of us are asleep. Perhaps we are blind to the reality that God is closer to us than we can fathom. We fret and worry because we feel alone or abandoned. But the apostle Paul tells us that in God "we live and move and have our being" (Acts 17:28). Elsewhere in the Bible, as Jesus was leaving his disciples, he told them that he would always be with them.

My suspicion is that God is not the only one with us. Another great theologian, Teilhard de Chardin, said, "We are not human beings seeking a spiritual experience; we are spiritual beings having a human experience." My faith tradition refers to being "surrounded by a great cloud of witnesses" (Hebrews 12:1), and I'm not talking about tooth fairies. I'm talking about our loved ones—those who are watching over us and praying for us. In other words, there really is no separation, even in death—especially in death. There is a great cloud of witnesses surrounding us and cheering us on.

❦

My son Wendell was very close with his grandfather, Cheri's father, who the grandkids called "Pappy." Pappy was extremely supportive of all four of his grandkids. He went to all their sports games, dance recitals, piano recitals, school events, and plays. Wendell ended up focusing on musical theatre, so of course Pappy and Grammy never missed a show.

After graduating from college, Wendell worked constantly, doing shows in various parts of the United States. In 2018, he took a seven-month gig doing a show in Pennsylvania. Normally, Pappy would be making road trips to go see his grandson. But several years ago, both Pappy and Grammy started showing signs of dementia. Over the years, their health declined, both mentally and physically.

On Sunday, May 27, 2018, Pappy's body seemed to start shutting down. That night, we called Wendell in Pennsylvania, so he could say things to his Pappy by phone. The next morning, we called Pappy's only sibling, his sister Ozella, who lives in Missouri, so she could do the same. Soon after that phone call, on May 28, Pappy died and made his transition.

We held the funeral on a day that Wendell did not have a performance so he could fly to Savannah for the service. Before he flew back to Pennsylvania, I reminded him that Pappy can now be with him. "He can now experience your show in Pennsylvania. Nothing is holding him back now."

Pappy can now echo Chelsea's words, "I'll be flying tonight."

❦

And we can echo Christi's words and say, "We're going to miss you, Pappy."

"But no. You're still right here with us, aren't you?"

May we have the faith to see beyond touch and sight.

Study Questions

- Have you ever struggled with separation anxiety and/or panic attacks?

- In periods of discouragement and doubt, what most renews your courage and faith?

- Teilhard de Chardin said, "We are not human beings searching for a spiritual experience; we are spiritual beings having a human experience." What does this statement mean to you?

- Why is it that spiritual things are so often difficult to understand?

- Do you believe in an afterlife? If so, what do you think it will be like?

- Have you ever sensed the presence of a loved one who has physically died? (This happens more than people realize because many people are hesitant to share such experiences with others, concerned that they will be judged.)

- What will you remember most from this story?

THE CARETAKER

When I first became the minister at Asbury Memorial UMC, the congregation was very small and most of the members were elderly. It was difficult for the older folks to attend meetings at night during the week, so they were accustomed to having their Administrative Board meeting early on Sunday mornings before Sunday School and the worship service. This was very difficult for me because I also was serving another church that had its service at 9:30 a.m. So, we would have our board meeting at Asbury Memorial at 7:00 a.m. Then, I'd lead a worship service at Wesley Oak UMC at 9:30 and come back to Asbury for the worship service at 11:15 a.m.

The only good thing about the early meeting on Sunday was that we had the world's best breakfast. A man named Francis Brannen always prepared it.

Francis and his wife, Nell, had been longtime members of Asbury Memorial. Nell was one of the great matriarchs of the church. She sang in the church choir, served on the Administrative Board, sewed with the Busy Bees, polished brass with the Altar Guild, and served as president of the

United Methodist Women and chair of the Church Bazaar, among other things. In other words, the church was her life.

Francis was a male version of Nell. He did just as many things, but he was not quite as vocal. He did them in a quieter manner.

Francis reminded me of Alfred Pennyworth, Bruce Wayne's loyal and tireless butler in the *Batman* series— classy-looking, quiet, always there. Alfred was Bruce's moral anchor, while providing comic relief with his dry sense of humor. Likewise, Francis was my moral anchor, while providing comic relief with his dry sense of humor. I appreciated Francis' biblical and theological knowledge and the dry wit that went with it.

Besides being the cook for the church, Francis was also the Sunday School teacher. Normally, I would be hesitant to send young visitors to a Sunday School class taught by an elderly man. But I never felt that way at Asbury Memorial. In fact, I would love to send them there because Francis had a deep, progressive theology. It was fun seeing these young people come out of the class amazed by what this man thought and taught.

After teaching the Sunday School class, Francis would shift over to the sanctuary, where he would become the head usher for the worship service. This was especially when he transformed into Alfred the butler, greeting people with warmth and grace in his dignified manner.

Francis had one other role at the church that made a great impact on us. He was chief decorator of the sanctuary. When we had poinsettias for the Christmas Service and when we had lilies for the Easter Service, Francis was in charge of placing them all. It was quite an undertaking for one person, especially at his age. But he always did it with quiet grace and dignity. And the poinsettias and lilies were always absolutely beautiful.

❦

When I was an associate minister at Wesley Monumental UMC in 1992, the minister from Asbury Memorial called and asked if I would preach for her one Sunday, which happened to be the Sunday before Christmas—the Sunday when churches place poinsettias in their sanctuaries. As I stood up to preach, I looked out at the very sparse crowd of the dying congregation, and I felt love and appreciation from them. The sanctuary was beautiful because of the Christmas poinsettias. They had done a wonderful job of making the old sanctuary space beautiful.

At that time, I had no idea that it was basically the work of one person, Francis Brannen. When I saw the magnificent sanctuary and the small but caring congregation, the experience planted a seed. It was the first time I thought that I would love to be part of helping a congregation like this.

A year later, when I heard that the denomination was planning to close the church due to its small and ageing congregation, I asked if I could be appointed there.

I joined them in June of 1993. Some of the members were homebound or in nursing homes, but most of them were faithfully attending church on Sundays. Each of them served and helped in their own unique way. Francis and Nell were viewed as their spiritual leaders.

In 2000, Nell suddenly died at home from a heart attack at the age of eighty-one. It was very difficult for Francis at first. But Francis, who was eighty-two at the time, continued being active at the church. As he approached ninety, he started slowing down. He moved out of his house and moved into Habersham House, an assisted-living facility.

❦

Asbury Memorial's sanctuary was built in 1921 and 1922. The congregation had not been able to maintain and repair it over the years so it had many issues. Besides the cracks in the walls and ceilings and the leaking roof, the air conditioning system and boiler did not work well. We also learned that termites had been feasting on our balcony and that only the plaster was holding it up. People also complained of a mold problem and feeling sick after worshipping with us.

Something had to be done. We would need to have a major capital-improvement plan and raise close to two million dollars—this during a recession! Amazingly, the money came in, and we completed the project in 2009. The sanctuary was spectacular, but Francis had never seen it.

One day in 2009, I went to see Francis. He had not been able to attend church for many months. He was now ninety-two and moving very slowly. He was also about ninety-five percent deaf. Anytime I went to see him during these later years, I took a writing pad. Since his mind was sharp and he could read well, I wrote things down to make it easier for us to communicate. On this particular day, I had a special surprise for him—large pictures of the renovated sanctuary.

I knew this fellow who had served the church so faithfully as decorator, head usher, Sunday School teacher, and chef would be interested in seeing them. In fact, he deserved to see them. Without his efforts and the efforts of our other older members, the church never would have had the chance for revitalization and renovation. Plus, Francis was a Georgia Tech graduate and had had a career as chief engineer at Kaiser Agricultural Company. With his background and training, I was interested in knowing what he thought about the layout and how everything looked.

When I went to his door and knocked, there was no answer. This didn't surprise me because Francis had lost his hearing. I opened the door and looked in. Sure enough, there he was in the second room, the back room of the apartment. He was sitting in his wheelchair watching television, his back to me. I knew he couldn't hear the television, so he was just watching the pictures on the screen. I went up to him gently, trying not to scare him, and greeted him.

When I showed him the pictures, his face lit up. He was thrilled. He asked question after question. After I would give responses on the writing pad, he would smile and give me a thumbs up. He seemed to be very pleased with everything about the project. We spent about thirty minutes examining the pictures. I put the pictures back into the big envelope, placed them on a shelf in his room, and said good-bye.

Before I could leave that section of Habersham House, I needed to get a code for the locked door of the building from the nurse's station. After giving me the code, the nurse asked if, on my way out, I would let Francis know that it was time for supper.

I went back to Francis' room and knocked on the door. Just like the time before, there was no answer. I opened the door, and he was again in the back room in his wheelchair. But this time he wasn't watching television. He had gotten the pictures off the shelf and was looking at them again. He had them up close to his face, so he could slowly examine every little inch of the beautiful space. He couldn't get enough of it. You could tell that he was so thankful that he had lived long enough to see this day.

Just several weeks after that visit, Francis became ill and moved to Hospice House. His son Bob and Bob's wife, Jenny, had gone out of town to take their grandkids to Disney World. While there, they got the news on Saturday, December 19, that Francis was not doing well.

I got a call letting me know that Francis had taken a turn for the worse and that it looked as though he would not be with us much longer. I quickly went over to Hospice House to be with him. Sitting on the bedside table right beside Francis was a small, but beautiful arrangement of flowers. On the vase was a notecard with the Asbury Clown. The flowers reminded Francis that his church family was praying for him and that the God he worshipped at Asbury Memorial was with him and would be taking good care of him.

I was with Francis for a couple of hours, offering prayers and softly singing some hymns. But I needed to leave to prepare for Sunday's Service the next day. I called church member Barry Parker to let him know about the situation because Barry had visited Francis on occasion. Barry lived in Port Wentworth, Georgia, but when he heard that Francis' family was out of town, he got in his car and drove twenty miles to take over for me. Several hours later, Barry called to tell me that Francis had made his transition and that he had been able to be with him.

Francis' son, Bob, was very thankful that Barry was able to be with his father when he made his transition. Bob said that when he got the call at Disney World about his father's death, the theme park serendipitously started playing his mother's favorite Christmas carol, "Silver Bells."

The next morning, I walked into the sanctuary and had another wow moment. The sanctuary was filled with beautiful Christmas poinsettias. It was December 20th, the Sunday before Christmas—the day that Francis always decorated the church. His successor, Randy Canady, did a fabulous job placing the flowers. Francis would have been proud.

Sister Joan Chittister has said, "A seed never gets to see the flower." Francis' wife, Nell, worked so hard at Asbury Memorial and didn't get to see the full bloom of the incredible church that it has blossomed into. Fortunately, Francis lived long enough to see and experience it. For this, we are thankful. And we are thankful that Francis was willing to be the cook, the teacher, the usher, and the decorator during the church's difficult years, so that those who pass through Asbury Memorial's doors in the future would be blessed.

One of Asbury Memorial's members, Helen Downing, introduced me to "The Bridge Builder," a poem that her father, Yank Dean, loved. Whenever I read it, I think of Francis and the way he lived. I offer it for your contemplation on the next page.

The Bridge Builder

An old man going a lone highway,
Came, at the evening cold and gray,
To a chasm vast and deep and wide.
Through which was flowing a sullen tide
The old man crossed in the twilight dim,
The sullen stream had no fear for him;
But he turned when safe on the other side
And built a bridge to span the tide.

"Old man," said a fellow pilgrim near,
"You are wasting your strength with building here;
Your journey will end with the ending day,
You never again will pass this way;
You've crossed the chasm, deep and wide,
Why build this bridge at evening tide?"

The builder lifted his old gray head;
"Good friend, in the path I have come," he said,
"There followed after me to-day
A youth whose feet must pass this way.
This chasm that has been as naught to me
To that fair-haired youth may a pitfall be;
He, too, must cross in the twilight dim;
Good friend, I am building this bridge for him!"

— Will Allen Dromgoole (1860-1934)
The Poetry Foundation

215

WOW! Wisdom

The people in the list below were members of Asbury Memorial when I arrived in June of 1993. Some of them were homebound or in nursing homes, but most of them faithfully attended worship services. We are thankful for these "bridge builders" who prepared the way for the congregation's revitalization and growth.

Mary Adams
Annette Anderson
Willie Beasley
Betty Beldin
Francis and Nell Brannen
Anna Butler
Naomi Byrn
Corine Cave
Carolyn Compton
Jane Corbin
Eunice Cox
John Crawford
Fannie Dasher
Marjorie Edenfield
Myrtle Gillins
Edna Girard
Pauline Grayson
Nell Hagins
Pearl Harley
Mary Hinely
Virginia Holliday
David and Frances Howe
Joe and Eunice Hunnicutt
Edna Jewett
Wiley and Myra Kessler

Elizabeth Lariscy
Elizabeth Martin
Mac and Thelma McDonald
Eileen Nall
Jewel Nieuwstraten
Thelma Norwood
Bernard Overstreet
Gwen Parker
Sarah Petway
Elsie Rutherford
Frank and Grace St. George
Wade Seyle
Carolyn Smith
Bertie and Gladys Spell
Celeste Stafford
Jean Stewart
Doris Taylor
Ida Thompson
Mary Emma Tolbert
Lerah Upchurch
Harold and Louise Wiley
Hazel Wingfield
Wallace Winn
Jack and Blannie Yirak
Robbie Hicks, the custodian

STUDY QUESTIONS

- What ways do you serve at your church?

- Do you find it depressing or encouraging that "a seed often doesn't get to see the flower"? Why?

- What bridges did Francis and Nell build for those who came after them?

- How do you think you will be remembered after you die?

- What bridges are you building for those who follow you? Physical bridges? Financial bridges? Emotional bridges? Spiritual bridges?

- What have your forebears passed on to you spiritually?

- If you have children or plan to have them, what would you like to pass on to them? How would you pass these things on?

- What will you remember most from this story?

ABOUT THE AUTHOR

Billy Hester has been senior minister of Asbury Memorial United Methodist Church in Savannah, Georgia, since 1993. He received a BFA in Theatre from Valdosta State College in 1981. After having a theatrical career in New York, he attended Princeton Theological Seminary, where he received a Master of Divinity in 1989. He then served at Marble Collegiate Church, the church of Dr. Norman Vincent Peale, in New York City before moving back to his hometown of Savannah, Georgia, where he has served at Wesley Monumental UMC, Wesley Oak UMC, and Asbury Memorial UMC. He and his wife, Cheri, have four adult children: Chelsea, Christi, Wendell, and Wesley.

At www.asburymemorial.org, you will find information about Billy's Asbury Memorial ministry, with video segments from the worship services, including his inspiring sermons.

Billy's publishing website is www.billyhesterbooks.com This book and Billy's first book, *Wow! Moments*, are both available there.